MEdiA
Generations

Media Allocation in a
Consumer-Controlled Marketplace

MEdiA
Generations

Media Allocation in a
Consumer-Controlled Marketplace

Martin P. Block, Ph.D., Don E. Schultz, Ph.D. & BIGresearch

PROSPER

Media Generations: Media Allocation in a Consumer-Controlled Marketplace
by Martin P. Block, Ph.D., Don E. Schultz, Ph.D. & BIGresearch

Copyright © 2009 by Prosper Business Development Corporation

ISBN 978-0-9819415-1-6

Library of Congress Control Number 2008942267

Printed in the United States of America

10 9 8 7 6 5 4 3 2 1

Published by Prosper Publishing
Web site: www.goprosper.com

Prosper Publishing books are available at special quantity discounts to use for sales promotions, employee premiums, or educational purposes. To order or for more information, please call 614-846-0146 or write to Prosper Publishing, 450 West Wilson Bridge Road, Suite 370, Worthington, OH, 43085.

Cover and Interior Book Design by Sun Editing & Book Design (www.suneditwrite.com)

Dedication

We have one man to thank for the modern advertising business—John Wanamaker. In the 1870s, this visionary Philadelphia merchant created the city's first department store, complete with price tags to eliminate haggling. Seeking to promote his new venture, he bought space in local newspapers. It was a smart move, and Wanamaker proved to be a marketing genius. However, early on, the "father of advertising" perceived a now oft-repeated truth about the business: "Half the money I spend on advertising is wasted. The trouble is, I don't know which half."

This book is dedicated to the advertising professionals and marketers who, for over 130 years, have been trying to figure out which half is wasted.

—P. R. R.

Contents

Foreword vii

1. Media Allocation in a Customer-Controlled Marketplace 1

2. Where Did All This New Stuff Come From? BIGresearch's
   Simultaneous Media Usage (SIMM) Studies 13

3. How Knowing Media Consumption Changes Media Planning 27

4. Media Generations 43

5. Media Usage 67

6. Media Influence 95

7. Allocating Media by Influence 109

8. Summary 121

About the Authors 127

Foreword

This book represents the completion of a twenty-five-year journey. More importantly, it sets out an alternative to the antiquated media allocation process that still dominates the marketing world. That process may have worked fifty years ago, but it is hopelessly unsuited to contemporary media consumption. This book demonstrates why — and what we can do about it!

Many have realized that there is a media allocation problem — for example, the way message distribution is still considered more important than message consumption — but mostly business has continued as usual. This book is the work of a team who looked at the problem and didn't just shrug their shoulders. Rather, they visualized a solution — to measure what consumers do and think, not what the marketer expects, predicts or hopes they will do and think.

This journey to put the consumer at the heart of media allocation began for me in 1983. I'd just left the RAB (Radio Advertising Bureau), where I'd been a frustrated regional manager, unhappy with the organization's emphasis on national business. I saw that we needed a consumer-centric media measurement service, and I persuaded one of the country's largest retail consulting firms to let me create one. The result was a new media marketing division that aimed to bridge the gap between retail and media by focusing on the people who shop for products—consumers.

In the course of marketing the new consumer-centric media model, I had some interesting encounters. I met then budding entrepreneur Jim Carnegie at the RAB annual sales conference. He was just launching *Radio Business Report* (*RBR*), the now-famous media publication designed to bring new business thinking to the radio industry, and he would prove an early and long-term advocate of consumer-centric sales techniques.

During a meeting with the SVP of research at a major radio group owner, I was given a glimpse of a service the group had developed to measure consumers for media outlets. The service was not only innovative in design and methodology, but also competitive. It allowed media outlets to sell consumer value instead of gross audience estimates. However, the group was reluctant to commit to the media measurement service, leaving the way open for someone else. Despite the risk, I jumped at the chance to acquire the service, and Impact Resources was formed in 1985.

My cofounder was Phil Rist, who left his position in M&A at a large broadcast group to join me, and together we helped make Impact Resources one of the country's fastest growing research organizations. Recognition for our consumer-centric approach soon followed: *RBR* named us "Rookie of the Year"; *Radio & Records* listed us in its annual "What's In What's Out" list as "In" (while listing Arbitron as "Out"); and *American Demographics* recognized Impact as one of the top 100 sources for information—a list that included the Census Bureau, Commerce Department and Nielsen. Soon, the National Association of Broadcasters' (NAB) radio audience measurement taskforce beckoned and, after a presentation from Impact, gave its verdict: "The [service] has great promise for radio broadcasters … we think your product is exciting and can benefit radio broadcasters."

Unfortunately, this marked the high point for Impact. The company's successful approach led to buyout offers and, ultimately, a hostile takeover by venture capitalists. The financiers' success proved short-lived, however, and Impact plunged into bankruptcy. Meanwhile, Phil and I, though exiled from the company we'd built, knew we wanted to continue to pursue our approach, with the best technological means available. It took time, but we returned in 2000 with a new e-mail-driven research firm—BIGresearch.

By May/June 2002, BIGresearch was conducting its first Simultaneous Media Usage™ (SIMM™) survey—with a sample of over 12,000 respondents. While developing SIMM, we encountered two academic and business marketing gurus: Don Schultz, who'd earned the title "Father of Integrated Marketing" for his books and work with leading marketers in the 90s; and, along with Don, his "numbers guy" Martin Block. Both were faculty members at Medill School at Northwestern University, where Martin was a master at translating Don's ideas into meaning by crunching the numbers.

In October 2002, *Advertising Age* introduced SIMM to the ad world. The following week, Don Schultz and Joe Pilotta gave the first BIGresearch public presentation, to an audience at the ARF (Advertising Research Foundation).

Phil, Don, Martin and I were working well, and we began to translate our robust consumer-centric media database into an allocation model. Along the way, three key presentations at the ARF, three more at the ESOMAR world audience measurement conferences—with articles in the *Journal of Consumer Behaviour* and the *Journal of Advertising Research* sandwiched in between—helped alert the market to SIMM's possibilities for achieving a truly consumer-centric holistic media service.

After seven years of development and market trials by BIGresearch clients and media planning practitioners, such as Jim Geoghegan at Media Head, the SIMM allocation media software was launched. And, we sincerely believe, media planning will never be the same!

We understood that the inherent nature of the business world is to resist change, just to go with the flow, so we sought out like-minded thinkers and kept our eye on the goal of making a difference by creating something better—by not accepting the status quo.

Along the way, we took risks and endured the barbs and criticisms of those who clung to the tried-and-failed methods, but we never quit. As a result, the media world will never be able to go back to business as usual. The journey is over. Change has finally come.

Gary Drenik
CEO
BIGresearch

Chapter

1

Media Allocation in a Customer-Controlled Marketplace

This volume is the first in a series of monographs describing a new set of strategies, tools and techniques designed to improve and enhance media planning and implementation for major consumer products companies and their distribution systems (generally, retail firms). The concepts and approaches described and defined are based on new research findings on how audiences consume media and media content. These findings, therefore, provide new insights into how marketing organizations and their agencies should consider, develop and implement brand communication programs with customers and consumers in, what we define as, the "customer-controlled marketplace."

By customer-controlled, we simply mean the traditional era of dominant media systems—one in which media organizations accumulated audiences based on content development and availability, and then sold advertisers time or space to access those audiences — is no longer the principal marketplace format. Instead, consumers now access and accept (or ignore) a multitude of media forms and formats, based on their own needs, desires, wishes and capabilities. Thus, the control of the media marketplace has clearly shifted. Consumers, as they always have, control the media forms they choose to use. The primary difference is that the alternatives available to them have increased exponentially.

Along with that shift in consumer behavior has come the need for new, improved and more relevant media planning, allocation and purchasing approaches that recognize those changes and provide new concepts and methodologies on how to deal with those changes.

The methods and approaches described in this volume have been derived from data gathered by BIGresearch in the U.S. over the past six years through its syndicated SIMM™ (Simultaneous Media Usage™) research studies. In total, the BIGresearch database presently consists of more than 170,000 individual consumer responses to how people consume and use a broad array of both traditional and emerging media. The BIGresearch methodology is detailed in Chapter 2.

The primary task of this volume is to help explain why and how the traditional methods of media planning, allocation and measurement are essentially obsolete, particularly in the United States and perhaps around the world. There is little question that the historical approaches developed and used over the past 40 or so years were effective in their time, namely, when mass media was the primary communication tool of the marketing organization and consumers aggregated to consume those media forms in large numbers. The SIMM data shows the major changes that have occurred over the past four years, which make those tools and techniques questionable and perhaps even irrelevant.

In this volume, we suggest why change is needed and provide a radically new set of media planning, allocation and measurement tools, which, we believe, will not only help marketing organizations improve the returns on their media investments, but will also assist them in moving to a new approach to media usage.

On the following pages, we outline how marketing organizations must begin to work with their customers and prospects, their channels and, indeed, the increasing number of people and firms who influence end-user decisions in co-creating effective and useful marketing communication programs for all parties. In short, this book outlines a media planning, allocation and measurement revolution that is becoming increasingly necessary, certainly in the United States.

In other volumes, we will detail how different and unique media planning is, or should be, in other markets, particularly China where the SIMM system has been in place since 2006. For the moment, however, we will focus only on the U.S., which continues to be the largest advertising media market in the world.

It's All About Change

This book is about change: media change and changes in media. Change is something many people talk about, but something in which few are, or want to be, involved. Humans are creatures of habit. We find things that work for us—a favorite food, an easy commuting route, a pair of well-worn jeans or a business solution—and, because they have worked in the past, repeat them. It's the ingrained habits that drive much human behavior—right or wrong. And, that seems to be especially true in marketing communication, particularly media planning, allocation and measurement.

So, in spite of all the hoopla about the subject of media fragmentation, media diffusion and the like, changing existing techniques, methodologies and approaches is hard. It's particularly difficult, if it involves changing ideas, concepts, approaches or methodologies that have worked in the past. No one wants to give up a proven "winner." So, we hang on to systems that are comfortable and familiar, even if they are obsolete and unrelated to the actual marketplace.

It seems change is especially hard for media people. "Media planning and allocation" has been more a static system than a changing one over the past couple of decades. For example, television ratings are still based on programs, not commercials. We still measure OTS (opportunities to see) not actual viewing. We use measures of advertising message distribution, not consumer consumption, that is, those messages seen and acted upon. We carefully track how inexpensively messages can be distributed, but fail miserably at estimating or calculating the returns on those investments. We value advertising success based on industry "awards" and peer acclaim, not on marketplace success. The trade press continues to equate media spending and marketplace success, in spite of the fact that the largest advertisers are now in major economic decline. The list could go on and on…hoary approaches and methodologies that continue to be used long after their appropriateness has disappeared.

Yet, these traditional systems are still used, acted upon and sometimes even venerated, seemingly because it's "what we have always done," or "they are the industry norm," or "they have currency in the marketplace." In most cases, however, it's clear that too many managers are simply afraid to try something new, to move away from the pack and abandon the industry norms.

Marketers, communicators and media gurus, in spite of all their proclamations of being "new, innovative, different or change agents," are generally loath to change—hanging on to the known, the accepted, the established. What the herd has done or is doing or is saying is considered okay. Or, worst of all, they repeat previous activities simply because they are safe and acceptable and can get management approval.

It's like Proctor & Gamble Company (P&G) and "slice-of-life" (SOL) television commercials. SOL worked in the past. Brand managers cut their teeth on the format. Everyone knows how to do one. There are piles of success stories. But "Marge talking over the back fence to Sally, her neighbor, about challenging cleaning chores" seems somewhat dated in the age of MySpace, Facebook, YouTube and other social networks. However, the airways continue to be filled with hardly believable slices-of-life, not only from P&G, but also from the thousands of look-alike marketers who copy the conglomerate's every move. It's "best practices of the past" run amok.

Change is hard to do. Particularly in marketing, advertising and communication, all those activities that are supposed to encourage, glorify, yea, even revere change.

So, today, we have embedded marketing communication systems in which change is difficult, if not impossible.

And, the very people who glorify change—the trade publication editors and reporters, the new media bloggers, the platform-trotting speakers at major industry association meetings—are the most difficult to change. Look at the agenda and subjects at media conferences and seminars: the same people with the same platitudes, preaching the same traditional tried-and-true approaches, justifying the same traditional approaches.

In 2004, Jim Stengel, then global marketing manager of P&G, said the "media advertising model is broken, it has to be fixed." Four years later, what has changed? Not much. Media is still wedded to reach and frequency, Gross Rating Points (GRPs), optimization models and the raft of other old-line, traditional media approaches, which have been in use for nearly fifty years.

When media reform is attempted, the traditional methods and approaches are found to be set in stone—hierarchy of effects models based on outdated and disproved learning models; optimization models based primarily on message distribution efficiency; linear planning methodologies in what is increasingly a networked world; and blinder-based views of consumer behavior. For the most part, the media planning, allocation and measurement approaches used today were developed in the 1960s and 1970s and haven't been updated. The methodologies, tools and techniques still being used are old-fashioned and outdated, but, because they are in place, are venerated and supported by marketers, agencies and particularly the media itself.

So, change is difficult in marketing, advertising and media businesses that should glorify change.

This volume, however, is about change. Lots of change. Some big changes, some small, but all relevant in a consumer-controlled marketplace.

This monograph deals with challenging, and perhaps even destroying, many advertising and media shibboleths. Because they challenge industry tradition and what is accepted as common knowledge, our findings often seem to slay sacred cows. Most of all, though, they question the business models used by many of the leading lights in market research, agency management, media planning and measurement and, most particularly, the industry mavens and the legions of suppliers who have developed very profitable businesses designed to resist change—certainly change in the way advertising media is planned, developed, implemented and, most of all, measured.

So, consider this fair warning.

If you're willing to consider change, read on.

If not, put this book aside, gather some comfortable friends and business associates and reflect nostalgically about how the business has always been, should continue to be or how you'd like it to be. Maybe tell a few stories about the "good old days." Recall some episodes of *Mad Men* and three-martini lunches. Hope the Internet, Web, social networks, TiVos and the like will go away. Feast on the past, for that is where media planning, allocation and measurement exists—in the past, not in the present and certainly not in the future.

It's Not Nice

This book is challenging, disturbing and radical. Written by out-of-the-box thinkers and researchers, it raises questions about how you've run your business, or recommended others run their businesses, for years. It may provide evidence that the industry has been wrong. And, though based on what the self-proclaimed "experts" say and do, it likely has been wrong for some time.

This book will particularly challenge how media funds are allocated. That is, how the media planner decides where to invest the marketer's scarce advertising and promotion dollars. The current system, based on typical efficiency allocation models that are increasingly statistically sophisticated, is all about sending out messages through various forms of fairly traditional media, notably television.

Our discussion in this text focuses, however, on how consumers receive advertising messages, take them in, process them and use them. It's about where consumers spend their media time, not where advertisers spend their media dollars. In short, the approaches we discuss are the opposite of what media planning, allocation and measurement have been about for decades.

Most of all, this book will likely raise questions of relevancy. Relevancy in what you think you know about how advertising and media work, or should work. And, that's the greatest risk. Finding you and your ideas are out of date or behind the times. No one wants to be told they are irrelevant, even if they are. So, how thick is your skin?

What This Book Is About

The first thing is that this book is about customers. Not advertisers or marketers or media or even gurus. It's not even about media or commercials or promotions. It's what the title says "Media Allocation in a Consumer-Controlled Marketplace." In other words, it's about how audiences use media forms, how many they use, in what combinations, at what times of day, and so on. And, it's not about small groups — it's not about watching a few people sit in front of a TV set in an artificial setting. It's about large numbers of people reporting what they do, how they do it, when they do it and how often they do it. And, it's about reports on people over time. The data in this report has been gathered for six years, so we're able to spot trends and change—something point-in-time measures, no matter how sophisticated, simply can't do.

Most importantly, these media usage measures are about not just media usage, they're also about how that media usage is connected to retailers, stores, products and services that people buy. What is important about these consumers is that they're the ones driving the entire economic system. They are the ones who make the marketing and communication business possible. Consumers create the income flows for marketing organizations. These are the people or firms who reach down in their purses, trousers or bank accounts and lay money on the table to acquire products and services they think, hope or dream will improve their lives, their businesses or, at least, their current situations. These are products and services they likely learned about through some type of promotional process, perhaps even through media advertising. For them, the changes need not necessarily be big or awesome or revolutionary. They're not looking for shock and awe from products and services, nor from the media forms that tell them about those products and services. Consumers can often be satisfied in seemingly insignificant ways they think are worthwhile.

Consumers want change, variety, something new. Marketers resist change. They want loyal customers who buy and continue to buy what they can make, efficiently and profitably. So, there is an inherent dichotomy in the entire marketing system. And who do you think will win? Our bet is on the consumers.

Consumers are a real problem for marketers. They're fickle and changeable and, in many cases, not the least bit interested in what the marketer has to say. They don't attend to the media the marketer has bought. Or, they multitask and completely destroy media measurement systems. Most of all, they're dynamic. They continue to change, evolve, morph and adapt to their changing life situations and the media environment around them. Marketers want stability. Customers seek change. So, number one, this book is about customers—the people who drive the marketing system. They are the ones who are changing, even if the marketers are not.

Second, this book is about communication and media systems. Not just the traditional outbound, marketer-controlled systems developed over the past fifty to seventy-five years. Instead, it's about the new "push-pull" systems that have emerged in the past dozen or so years. The Internet, Web, mobile telephony, Short Message Systems (SMS) video games, social networks and a host of other communication forms are increasingly being used by consumers and melded into their communication usage patterns. And those are being combined with all the traditional outbound, "push" systems on which marketers have relied for years. So, this book is about the new integrated, aligned and comprehensive systems that customers are using more and more, every day. And with which most marketers continue to struggle, trying to fit their established approaches to a new type of communication marketplace.

Third, this book is about new ways of thinking about marketing and communication messaging—from the customer's, not the marketer's view. It's about how customers use media today: whether they are monochromic or polychromic information processors, that is, how they process information, sequentially or in parallel; whether they are digital natives or digital immigrants; how they multitask, in multiple media forms, shifting from foreground to background media forms and back again in the wink of an eye. It's about how people use media-delivered marketing communication, not how marketers distribute it—media consumption, not media distribution. It's the real world of media and media usage, not the one found in the media optimizer models agencies have dreamed up about how the world should be.

This book is based on what is happening in the marketplace: what customers are doing, not what marketers are trying to protect.

Fourth, this text is about how advertising and media should be planned and implemented. Not the top-down "we're smarter than you are, you dumb customer," but from the bottom up. Customers know what they're doing and why they're doing it. They may not be able to articulate the reasons using the standard survey questionnaires and lingo, but they know, or at least they have justifications for their actions. They know because it's their lives that are being impacted based on the advertising they see, the purchases they make, the commitments they engage in and the rationales they create for themselves, not just the bottom line of the marketing organization.

Finally, this book is about new thoughts on what people actually do in the marketplace. Most marketing theory and practice is based on behaviorist psychology, developed more than a century ago; thoughts, ideas, postulations and propositions about how humans think and behave. The content you'll find on the following pages, challenges the traditional stimulus-response models on which media planning is based. With conditioned-consumer-behavior, behavioral changes are assumed to result from attitudinal change, and the still-existing beliefs that message frequency and repetition are the most critical factors in marketing communication success. In short, increasing evidence shows that the assumptions, hypotheses and beliefs that marketers have developed over the years on how the human brain works and how marketers should or could use that information to influence future consumer behaviors are wrong-headed, misplaced or simply inaccurate.

New neural knowledge is challenging many of the traditional marketing and communication concepts. And it's not just how the human brain works, but how that impacts message acquisition, retention and application. Those are areas many media people have seemingly ignored in the pursuit of message distribution. Much of what you'll find in the following chapters is derived from new information. That information comes from looking at the marketplace in a different way: starting with customers rather than starting with the markets or media systems or media models.

Why start with consumers? That's easy. Many of today's real experts say we've learned more about how the human brain works in the past five years than in the previous five hundred. That's important, for it is within the human brain that all marketing and communication activities, actions and results occur. It's the springboard for accountability, for it's where consumer decisions are made, which are then reflected in marketplace behaviors. If advertising messages aren't processed, because they aren't seen, then no matter how sophisticated the media planning models are, it is all for naught.

Don't be concerned, however. This isn't a clinical tome on brain waves and frontal lobotomies. It's about what BIGresearch has observed, had reports of and learned about how marketing and communication works in today's push-pull marketplace. And, all that information has come from customers and prospects. That's what makes it so interesting and so valuable.

Some of the findings and the way they are reported on the following pages will be disturbing. Others merely at variance with what you always thought you knew or what you have accepted as common industry knowledge. Some will reinforce your own intuition. And still others will require some thoughtful contemplation to generate their full meaning. But they will give you a new view of marketing, marketing communication, advertising, promotion and, most of all, media and media planning—all those things a seller does to try and influence a buyer.

So, if you have a deep down, gut-wrenching feeling that things aren't right in your marketing and media communication programs, read on. The following pages will likely confirm that intuitive sense. At least you will be alerted to the changes and challenges that you're going to face, not just tomorrow, but, today.

On the other hand, if you happen to be one of the naysayers, and wish this entire media discussion would simply go away, give this book to a friend. At least someone will profit from the new knowledge that follows.

Chapter

2

Where Did All This New Stuff Come From? BIGresearch's Simultaneous Media Usage (SIMM) Studies

The content of this monograph is based on the research studies of BIGresearch, Columbus, Ohio. The primary studies used are the Simultaneous Media Usage (SIMM) studies, which have been ongoing since October 2001. The data has been collected via online surveys, conducted twice yearly with panels that represent nationally projectable samples of the entire U.S. population. The respondent base in the studies now totals over 170,000 individual responses so trending and longitudinal analysis are possible.

SIMM is one of the three BIGresearch syndicated products. One is Consumer Intentions and Actions™ (CIA). This survey monitors the reactions of over 8,000 consumers per month to determine their purchasing activities and intentions for the future. It delivers fresh, demand-based information on where the retail consumer is shopping and their changing behavior. CIA is conducted monthly. It has been conducted since October 2001, so there are now more than 82 data sets in the repository.

A third product of BIGresearch is the China Quarterly. This is an online survey of Chinese consumers in the 18–34 age range. It mirrors much of the data being collected through the U.S. SIMM studies and portions of the CIA approach as well.

In this monograph, we use only SIMM data collected in the U.S. Later monographs will compare and contrast some of the CIA and China Quarterly studies with the SIMM studies.

What Is SIMM?

The syndicated Simultaneous Media Usage (SIMM) study provides a tool for understanding the inter-relationships of consumer multiple media usage activities—such as time spent per medium, media usage combinations and most influential media forms—all of which impact marketing effectiveness and the Return on Investment (ROI) of marketer communication expenditures. SIMM data is available for specific retailers or targeted consumer groups through such differentiators as age, gender, income, lifestyle and geography.

The SIMM studies have been the basis for several media and media planning studies, papers and presentations. Schultz and Pilotta first presented a media planning model based on measures of audience media consumption, rather than media and marketer message distribution, using the proprietary BIGresearch SIMM database in 2004. (Schultz and Pilotta, 2004) Building on that model, Schultz, Pilotta and Block (Schultz, Pilotta and Block, 2005, 2006) illustrated how they had been able to populate the media consumption model, again using the online gathered consumer data from the SIMM database.

These media consumption models are based on (a) similar media usage by media form, (b) similar simultaneous media usage patterns and (c) similar impact or influence of media forms on purchase decisions as identified by various product categories.

The SIMM Database

The analyses, findings and methodologies that follow are based almost totally on the SIMM database. While the data has been gathered over the past six years (12 in total)—on a twice yearly basis—and there are now over 170,000 responses stored in the database. This allows researchers to develop trend analyses and compare various media forms over that period of time. Current tables shown in this monograph are primarily taken from the latest wave, dating from June 2008. Thus, the recommendations and approaches are current and usable in the marketplace.

All responses have been generated online based on a double opt-in e-mail consumer response methodology. The samples have been drawn using accepted online survey methods. The same approaches and methodologies have been employed over the entire six-year period. The surveys that make up the SIMM responses are anonymous and self-administered.

The questions asked are based on ten basic categories: demographics; leisure time; media influence on spending; frequency of purchases; Web site most often shopped; planned purchases in the next thirty days; media behaviors; census region; and other factors. The questionnaires are designed to be completed and returned very quickly.

BIGresearch data respondents are not paid for their participation. Rather, they participate in a quarterly contest for modest prizes. The questionnaire takes approximately ten to fifteen minutes to complete.

BIGresearch uses proprietary software that weights and balances all participants on the fourteen age and sex cells used in the U.S. Census. This assures a nationally representative sample in each wave.

Figure 1 shows the history of the first twelve waves of SIMM studies. The number of completed interviews included are shown by individual survey. Over 17,000 responses are included in the most recent wave. The number of variables collected has also increased dramatically over the history of the surveys. The first wave had just over 100, while the most recent wave over 1,000 variables.

FIGURE 1: SIMM History Completed Interviews and Variables Measured

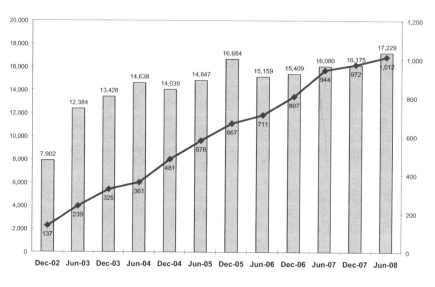

Source: BIGresearch

Of particular interest to media planners, buyers and researchers is the fact that each SIMM study is representative of the entire U.S. population. As Figure 2 illustrates, the most recent SIMM survey shows demographic characteristics that are very close to U.S. Census estimates, thus, confirming the representativeness of the SIMM data.

FIGURE 2: Selected Demographic Characteristics of SIMM (June 2008)

	Percent		Percent
Male	48.6	White	66.0
Female	51.4	Hispanic	12.5
Married	49.9	African-American	11.5
Children in household	32.8	Other	7.2
		Multiracial	2.8

Source: BIGresearch

Figure 3 shows the distributions by reported age and household income for the most recent SIMM wave conducted in June 2008. (The base for the analysis, approaches and recommendations which follow in this monograph.) The average age is just under 45 years, and the average household income is about $55,000.

FIGURE 3: Age and Income of SIMM (June 2008)

	Percent		Percent
18–24	13.1	Less than $15	7.9
25–34	17.9	15 to 25	8.9
35–44	19.4	25 to 35	12.2
45–54	19.2	35 to 50	16.2
55–64	14.0	50 to 75	21.7
65 and over	16.5	75 to 100	15.5
		100 to 150	12.1
		150 and over	5.5
Average	44.6	$54,559	

Source: BIGresearch

SIMM Media Consumption Characteristics

The SIMM database includes thirty-one media forms, ranging from over-the-air television to in-store signage to Web radio. This usage data is collected in each SIMM study, thus making time series analyses of changes in media usage over various periods possible and practical.

In addition to the media forms used, three unique media consumption and usage characteristics are tracked in each SIMM study:

- Experiential time—the individual consumption of media by person by dayparts. There are seven dayparts: 6–10 a.m., 10–noon, noon–4.30 p.m., 4.30–7.30 p.m., 7.30–11 p.m., 11 p.m.–1 a.m., and 1–6 a.m. This allows SIMM data to be compared and contrasted with traditional media measures.

- Simultaneity—the multitasking/overlapping of media consumption by consumer, that is, how media forms are consumed and in what combination at the same time. This enables the researcher and media planner to identify the potential synergy that might be possible through the purchase of possible media combinations during certain time periods. It also helps identify more accurately the actual media audience by medium. Traditional media measures are conducted on one media at a time, such as television only or radio only.

- Media engagement influence—the influence consumers report that an individual media form has on their product decisions in each of the measured product categories. In addition, since respondents also report their preferred retailers by product category, it enables the marketer to connect his or her media expenditures to channel and usage by consumers. This is a true, consumer-reported engagement measure, which identifies the value of the medium to the consumer in terms of the impact and effect it has on their purchase decisions. Thus, it moves beyond media engagement to media impact.

In addition to the media questions, many traditional demographic and leisure-time questions are asked. Thus, the questionnaire is quite comprehensive. For example, there are thirteen standard demographic and thirty-five leisure time questions in the survey instrument. These range from questions about individual and team sports to antique collecting to gambling.

Respondent use of media is a key element in the SIMM studies. Questions are asked regarding individual media usage, such as watching television, listening to music, making online purchases, using e-mail, blogging, and so on. In the thirty-one different forms of media covered in the questionnaire, nineteen deal with types of in-store media, thus, moving media consumption from the traditional forms of mass media to new measures that provide a comprehensive view of consumer media exposure and consumption.

A substantial amount of information on products and services is also obtained. Information regarding thirteen major product categories, consisting of thirty-seven specific products, is gathered in each survey. These are related to well over 266 specific retailer choices (that is, favorite retailer for the various product categories), along with thirty-nine automotive brands, more than fifty cable television channels, fifteen television formats, five newspaper categories, over fifty magazine titles, twelve search engine alternatives, thirty-five specific Web sites, ten video game platforms, twelve questions regarding disease states, and twenty-three spending and purchasing questions. In short, the SIMM data provides one of the most comprehensive views of consumers, their media usage and media consumption available.

Purchasing and SIMM Reported Data

There are other key elements in the SIMM database that relate specifically to individual purchase behavior, which expand the view of how consumers act and react in a multi-channel media world, such as:

- Competitive shopping and customer loyalty trends

- Six month purchase outlook and intent to purchase for soft goods by product category. In addition, frequency of product purchases is also gathered

- Consumer merchandise—purchased or planned

- Shopping trends

- Cross shopping behavior

- Search behavior and purchasing

- Fast food frequency

All of these are cross-tabulated with media consumption to provide a better view of customers and prospects and the impact media has on their purchasing habits.

Of critical importance to the development of the media consumption study are the questions that relate consumer choice of media use to media forms that most influence purchase decisions. These questions form the basis for the media-influence questions. There are eight merchandise categories to which these questions are applied:

- Groceries
- Apparel/clothing
- Electronics
- Medicine

- Eating out
- Telecommunications
- Car/truck purchases
- Home improvements

The thirty-one media alternatives used in the questionnaire are:

- Web site
- Word-of-mouth
- Television
- Cable
- Internet service provider (ISP)
- Broadband
- IPTV
- Search engine use
- Retail channel shopped
- Radio
- In-store promotion
- Article about product in media
- Newspapers
- Newspaper inserts
- Direct mail
- Magazine

- Internet advertising
- Outdoor billboards
- Picture phone
- Instant messenger
- E-mail advertising
- Yellow pages
- Satellite radio
- Text message
- MP3 player
- Web radio
- Video games
- Personal digital assistant (PDA)
- Cell phone
- Blogging
- TiVo

With this broad range of media forms used and their value to the consumer, plus, the ability to connect that data to past and planned purchases, the media planner and buyer has new views of consumers that have never before been possible.

Marketer and Retailer Interactions

Purchase intention by product category and preferred retailer are two areas that have been grossly neglected in current media planning and buying approaches. By including this information, media planners and buyers—representing retailers and/or manufacturers—can understand their customer's media usage behavior, purchase intent and the media-motivated sales that result. This is a major improvement over traditional media distribution-based models where only outbound numbers are available.

With the current interest by manufacturers in understanding their channels, finding a common ground for manufacturers and retailers to meet is likely more beneficial than looking at data produced by heat sensors or eye scans of customer traffic in store aisles.

With this media analysis approach, manufacturers are able to become much more consumer-centric, and are, therefore, better able to partner with their retail channels to facilitate product movement across all media, thus, connecting external media to in-store promotion.

A critical part of media consumption includes nineteen types of in-store promotional media, which provides a holistic media consumption profile of consumers. This provides manufacturers with an opportunity to create intervention strategies within the various retail channels as needed. For example, the retail channels in the SIMM data can be viewed by region, by Metropolitan Statistical Area (MSA), by Designated Market Area (DMA) and, in some cases, by state and city. Additionally, the consumption scores of in-store media allow media planners to develop an in-store accountability model that addresses the customer, not merely an eye or an ear, as Cost per Thousand (CPM) generally does.

The BIGresearch Approach

A summary of the differences in the BIGresearch consumption-driven data approach and traditional methods of allocating media and marketing communication spending is shown in Figure 4. The biggest difference in the BIGresearch media consumption approach is the use of more media measures, especially those dealing with media influence. The measure is also consistent across all the media and marketing communication categories.

One of the primary values of the media consumption studies available through the SIMM research base is the possibility for the marketing manager and media planner to create better allocation models. Presently, most media allocation approaches are based on efficiency, that is, what media combinations provide the most efficient distribution of pre-determined messages. SIMM data and the use of consumer media consumption approaches, when combined with amount time spent with the media form, the influence of the various media on purchase decisions, the ability to identify media usage patterns and, at some point, media synergy moves the media planning game to the critically important area of effectiveness rather than simply the efficient distribution of messages.

It is believed the SIMM data can also be used to help develop forecasting models against which media purchases can be measured over time. In short, the use of SIMM data and the new approaches it provides, truly change the way media planning, purchasing and measurement is and will be conducted in the future.

In the chart below, we contrast the traditional measures of Return on Investment (ROI) made by organizations with the new Return on Customer Investments (ROCI), which are possible using the BIGresearch SIMM data. ROI is aggregated data, that is, only the total market response is known. In ROCI, this information can be related to specific customers or prospects. Clearly, knowing which consumers responded is a much more sophisticated measure of the impact and effect of the media investment than simply knowing that the "market" responded.

FIGURE 4: State-of-the-Art ROI vs. BIGresearch ROI

State-of-the-Art ROI	BIGresearch ROCI
Hierarchy of Effects/Tonnage Model The more media you buy, the more exposure. Given sufficient stimulus response, the consumer will have no choice but to buy.	**Consumption Model/Consumer-Centric** The consumer is in control in all decisions on purchasing and media.
Consumers Are Passive Consumers are a receptacle waiting for advertising to tell them what to do.	**Consumers Are Active** Consumers actively select, ignore or enhance the advertising they consume.
Historical Data All data is past-oriented — what has already happened. Assumes "what you did in the past is what you will do in the future."	**Synchronic Present and Future-Oriented** Data is present- and future-oriented, linked to what people will do next based on their typical everyday life patterns.
Historical Scorecard Results of historical data are a score based on what you already know: "Reading last night's baseball scores."	**Proactive Plan for Better ROI** Results of future-oriented data provide a plan of what is likely based on what the consumer says: "Knowing the box score before the game is played."
Mass Media Focus is media-centered, primarily on radio, television, print and trade promotions.	**Media Agnostic/31 Types of Media** No media are privileged. 31 different media are investigated. Consumers are seen as dynamic creatures.
Data Inputs Are Surrogates for Consumer Data such as price elasticity is used as a substitute for consumer data.	**Primary Consumption Data from Consumers** There is direct dialogue with consumers based on their reported media and purchasing habits.

State-of-the-Art ROI	BIGresearch ROCI
New Media Aggregated by Third Party Norms New media are summarized by an arbitrary measure to determine total new media expenditure.	**15 New Media Differentiated from Consumer Surveys** Consumer determines the measure of each medium on their purchase expenditures.
Impact of Media Measures by Silos Simultaneous media usage is ignored. Each medium, e.g., television, radio or print, is measured separately and independently.	**Holistic Media Measures** Simultaneous media usage and impact on purchasing are built in. This is based on what consumers do, not what the media does.

With this understanding of the SIMM database and the type of information available, it is now possible to move on to how this information can be used to develop better media planning and buying now and into the future.

References

Lavidge, Robert C., amd Gary A. Steiner, "A Model for Predictive Measurements of Advertising Effectiveness," *Journal of Marketing*, Vol. 25, October 1961, pp. 59-62.

Russell Colley, *Defining Advertising Goals for Measured Advertising Results*, New York: Association of National Advertisers, 1961.

Schultz, Don E. and Joseph J. Pilotta. "Developing the Foundation for a New Approach to Understanding How Media Advertising Works." 3rd ESOMAR/ARF World Audience Measurement Conference, June 13–18, 2005, Geneva.

Schultz, Don E., Joseph J. Pilotta and Martin P. Block. "Implementing a Media Consumption Model." 4th ESOMAR/ARF World Audience Measurement Conference, June 22–24, 2006, Montreal.

Schultz, Don E. and Jeffrey S. Walters. *Measuring Brand Communication ROI*. Association of National Advertisers, New York, 1997.

Wilbur Schramm and Donald F. Roberts, eds., *The Process and Effects of Mass Communication*, Urbana: University of Illinois Press, 1971.

Chapter

3

How Knowing Media Consumption Changes Media Planning

The approach to marketing communication media planning, and especially inter-media allocation decisions, using information from the SIMM studies is quite different from traditional approaches. As before, the approach begins with a consumer-centric model, rather than a media-centric approach.

A consumer-centric model is exactly what is needed in the new customer-driven marketplace. It simply means that organizations must understand that their guiding business practice must recognize the consumer has multiple choices in products and services and also has multiple media channels from which to select. The marketer does not own the customer, as has been the belief for so long, including the supposedly more sophisticated customer relationship management (CRM) systems which are now all the vogue. Rather, the customers and the various stakeholders actually and literally own the marketer's businesses, since they control the income flows to the firm. Thus, a consumer-centric approach is mandatory.

The daily time constraints of the consumer and the increasing fragmentation of the media are of significant importance to all marketers. It not only verifies the push-pull media marketplace, it helps explain the consumer's disconnect with traditional media forms. In short, it explains many of the changes currently seen in the media distribution and consumption models.

Thus, we start with a look at the conceptual differences between distribution and consumption as they relate to media communication channels.

Distribution Programs

Distributive approaches to resource mobilization require fundamentally different ways of organizing resources and management techniques relative to how those distribution systems are or can be maximized. Distributive approaches are typified by formal programs, tightly scripted specifications of activities, designed to be invoked by known parties in predetermined contexts. This would seem to closely resemble the present media distribution models and the advertising messages distributed through those media forms.

Consumption Channels

Consumption approaches, in contrast, can be implemented through various channels. They are designed to flexibly accommodate diverse providers and consumers of those resources. These channels are much more open-ended and have been designed to evolve, based on the participants' learning about their use and their own changing needs.

Figure 5 presents a comparison of push and pull models in more detail. It can be summarized as programs versus channels.

We argue that marketer media allocation approaches have been, historically, and still are, essentially distribution programs. What is needed in today's consumer-driven marketplace are consumption approaches. Thus, we see the apparent conflict between what marketers want to do, what consumers want to do and what both are actually doing.

FIGURE 5: Distributive Programs vs. Consumption Channels

Distributive Programs	Consumption Channels
Demand as controlled anticipation	Demand is highly variable
Centralized control	Decentralized initiative
Procedural	Modular
Tightly coupled	Loosely coupled
Resource-centric	People-centric
Participation restricted (few participants)	Participation open (many diverse participants)
Efficiency focus	Innovation focus

As shown in the chart above, traditional media planning approaches are essentially distributive programs. The marketer controls all the variables: determining what media will be purchased and in what amount; how often messages will be distributed; and designing the messages to achieve marketer goals. It is all based on an allocation of available funds, with participation limited to those consumers who use the media form the marketer has purchased.

Alternatively, what is needed in a consumer-controlled marketplace is a consumption channel approach. This system recognizes that demand is in the hands of the consumer; that it is modular, which means that the consumer determines what media will be consumed and in what combinations; that other people can be involved in the media form, as seen in the new social networks, such as Facebook; and that the system is essentially people-centric.

The reason the distributive approach was developed, and is still in use today, is that advertisers and media planners still assume individuals (consumers) are calculatively rational as well as acquisitive. It also assumes they have roughly accurate information about the market and are continuously seeking information or knowledge that will improve or enhance their personal well-being. Given these assumptions and the consumer's traditional paucity of easily available information, the marketer doled out product information as he or she saw fit through the media forms which were perceived to be the most efficient. Since the consumer had few other resources or information alternatives there was an ongoing consumer demand for product or service information. And because the marketer knew the consumer had a lack of market and product information and the consumer assumed that it would require time or money to acquire it, the consumer was willing to give up time to acquire the information the marketer made available through media advertising. This model has been the presumptive approach to mass market/mass media advertising for the past seventy-five or so years.

It All Comes from the "Four Ps"

The basic media advertising model is closely aligned to, and generally derived from, the "four Ps" marketing mantra. This management approach espouses the importance of product, price, place and promotion and gives no heed to the consumer or the situation in the marketplace. Thus, even though it is internally focused and assumes the goal is to dispose of the products the marketer has available it is the driving force in marketing management around the world.

As noted, consumers, customers, users or purchasers, that is, whoever buys and consumes the products or services, are ignored in the four Ps model. This is a problem that continues to grow in the push-pull marketplace surrounding marketers today.

The four Ps approach was developed in the late 1950s, and while there have been numerous marketplace changes, marketers have religiously held on to this "marketer-in-control" management approach. It assumes that if the four Ps are done right, customers will magically appear and will buy and continue to buy whatever the marketer is trying to vend.

A further assumption of the four Ps model is that the marketer and the media control the commercial marketplace. That is, when it comes to promotion, the fourth of the four Ps, the marketing organization is assumed to be in complete control of the system. The marketer develops the messages and incentives and then contracts with the various media organizations to distribute those messages through the media owner-controlled communication forms. This is a clearly outbound only, mass communication, efficiency-based approach.

The model assumes that distributing more messages is always in the marketing firm's best interests. Thus, there is a built-in incentive for marketers to overspend in media, assuming that more messages distributed is always better than fewer.

The current media model is supported by the three factors that are the foundation for present media planning methods.

Influences on Traditional Media Planning and Push Media Models

Three major factors greatly influenced media planning in its early stages and continue to dominate media planning to this day: a) mass communication theory, b) "hierarchy of effects" models and c) probability sampling techniques.

1. **Mass Communication Theory**

    Early advertising practitioners, and especially media planners and buyers, borrowed from mass communication theory to provide a basis for understanding media distribution and, thus, the diffusion of advertising messages.

The media planning model evolved from the Schramm and Roberts (1971) approach to explaining how mass media works. It presented the mass media as a simple, linear system in which the communicator selected the media form and the receiver received and accepted the messages sent.

Sender → Media → Receiver

As can be seen, the sender is always in control of the distribution system, a fact that is somewhat outdated in today's fragmenting media marketplace.

2. **"Hierarchy of Effects" Models**

Early media planners accepted and embraced the "hierarchy of effects" models developed by Lavidge and Steiner (1961) and Colley (1961). These provided a hypothetical series of measurable steps marketers could use to move consumers through on the way to a purchase decision. The simplified model looked like this:

Awareness→Knowledge→Preference→Conviction→Purchase

Both the Lavidge & Steiner and Colley hierarchy of effects models were based on the behavioral psychology that was in vogue at the time. The basic premise was that consumers could be trained to purchase, similar to the way Pavlov trained dogs or Skinner trained pigeons, namely, through conditioned-learning. It was a stimulus-response model that posited that the number of times the person saw the message (frequency) had a direct impact on how quickly they would respond to the marketer's offerings. Thus, there was an emphasis on message frequency, which worked to the advantage of the media organizations who charged for media message distribution.

The model was primarily focused on new customer acquisition, which was quite relevant at the time. As markets mature, however, acquisition becomes less and less important, being replaced by customer retention and growth. So, today, media planners are saddled with the models that were appropriate in the 1970s and 1980s, but, are less relevant today.

3. **Probability Sampling Techniques**

As the marketplace expanded and media forms accumulated larger audiences, media planners began relying on probability sampling techniques to identify the size and descriptors of the audience. Media evaluators began to use relatively small, statistically relevant samples of the entire population, then they projected the results of those samples to the entire universe. Thus, they were able to generalize and speculate on audience size, make-up and value. That's the same approach Nielsen uses today to define the viewing audiences of television programs.

This approach worked then because media audiences were fairly general, for example, women 18–49 or men 25–59. As markets fragmented, and marketers began to focus on more targeted audiences, consumption categories had to change to include more than age and sex. Gross audience estimates were no longer appropriate.

In addition, all audience size and make-up estimates were based on a normal distribution of the population, or what is called the "normal curve." For the most part, there are few normal distributions of populations in any marketing audiences or among any product purchasers. Thus, there is increasing concern on how relevant our statistical approaches and models are today. Upon investigation, one almost always finds the 80/20 rule prevailing or some variation on that idea of heavy users who dominate both brand purchases and product or service consumption.

None of these theories of mass media/mass communication or the hierarchy of effects were proven in the marketplace. While they make intuitive good sense, they lack any real substance, although they have been widely accepted by the marketing community, particularly media planners.

In addition, the systems described were all push or outbound oriented. The consumer was never part of the equation and the metrics, where they were used, referred to push, that is, outbound message distribution opportunities on the part of the marketer, such as CPM (cost per thousand) gross rating points (duplicated audiences), reach (unduplicated audiences), frequency (gross audience/reach), and so on. All served as surrogates for real consumers whom the media planner likely never saw nor with which they interacted.

These theories have been used as the basis to build econometric models to attempt to gage advertising impact, effects and return-on-investment models. They work from the hierarchy of effects model, using norms that measure the media, which then have the greatest amount of dollars allocated to them. Other media are then viewed in terms of whether they are capable of (or incapable of) providing incremental increases in audience size or scope.

Dealing with Dynamism

Dynamic market surveys, such as that provided by BIGresearch, which provides consistent and continuous media measures, is the solution to the push marketing tradition and allows movement toward a consumer-oriented pull approach. The historically difficult inter-media comparison problem is, therefore, readily solved by using the SIMM syndicated studies.

Because marketers are now recognizing that consumers and the marketplace are dynamic, in our computationally driven culture, we have witnessed the emergence of an increasing focus on networked and automated apparatuses to measure media engagement and the various arenas for security, combat and navigation. And, we have also seen the promulgation of the Personal People Meter (PPM), Pioneering Research for In-Store Metric (P.R.I.S.M.) and Radio Frequency Identification (RFID) technologies, all designed to measure or estimate the involvement of consumers and customers in the marketplace. For some marketers, these have now been nominated to be the ears and eyes for understanding the behaviors of consumers.

Yet, electronic surveillance techniques do not provide an understanding of the "whys" of consumer actions and activities. In fact, it is becoming apparent the closer the technology invades, the further it gets from human action. Thus, less intrusive methodologies and more insightful approaches are clearly needed.

With the multiple functions of the media comes the ever-present specter of surveillance through mobility. Twenty-first-century mobility techniques constitute a major threat to privacy. This is significant not only in regard to ethical and legal issues surrounding privacy, but technological resistance also creates its own inhibitions among consumers. For the reasons, participatory consumer research such as the SIMM data moves the marketer closer to the marketplace than ever before.

Evolving from the Push/Distribution Model of Advertising

The traditional assumption of the passive, predictable model of consumer consumption is clearly outdated. Consumption spending as measured now comprises roughly 70% of the gross national product (GNP), and it has typically been understood as passive and predictable. Spending on food, clothing, and typical non-durable goods has been taken for granted. It is assumed consumers go about their normal activities and are motivated and impacted by marketers activities.

This passive predictable model does not assume such spending to be completely constant. It has periods of disruption built in, such as war and inflationary times, and it takes into account other circumstances, such as seasonality, as well. For instance, swings in auto purchases might occur due to high costs or fears of gasoline shortages. However, during the normal course of things, counter to the passive predictable model, no matter how intense the wants may be, consumers still cannot buy more unless they have more income to make purchases. Of course, credit and borrowing on accumulated savings may provide a burst in spending, but the effect of that will always be limited by the reality of income and expenses. Clearly, a new model and new approach is needed.

Consumer-Centric Research: What Is It and Why Is It Important?

To understand and explain various consumer actions, the best approach is to investigate the typical everyday behavior of consumers. That would allow the marketer to understand the irregularities and anomalies often found in consumer purchasing behavior. Consumer-centric research is developed with the goal of understanding consumers' interests, intents, expectations and the resulting expenditures they make. The ideal situation for marketers would be to know how these concepts can or could be integrated into a media consumption and purchase action survey. In that way, continual consumer actions could be placed in the context in which they occur and thus provide the marketer with a realistic version of why consumer behavior occurs as it does.

Any type of consumer-centric understanding must take into account the values, norms and behavioral meaning of the consumer. Those would provide the context for consumer self-understanding and, therefore, the marketer's interpretation of those behaviors. Consumer action does not follow causes, however. Rather, it springs from valuations and norms of the competitive situation and collective behavioral expectations of the consumer and his or her relevant cohorts.

Unfortunately, many years ago, marketers, lacking this consumer-centric knowledge, sufficed with assumptions and hypotheses of how consumers behaved in the marketplace. They built their models in the mid-twentieth century using the various psychological concepts then in vogue. The basic approach, which still underlies most marketing and communication models, was the hierarchy of effects—two versions of which were popularized by Lavidge and Steiner and Colly in the early 1960s and were described earlier.

The hierarchy of effects model represents the traditional or push distribution model. It is shown in Figure 6 below.

FIGURE 6: Hierarchy of Effects Model

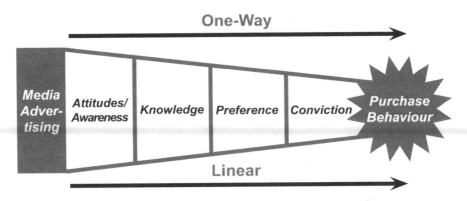

"Influencing and Persuading Customers"

It is important to note that most of the hierarchy of effects models stop short of the ultimate consumer response: purchase behavior. These models are focused only on what are called "communication effects," that is, what the marketer wants the consumer to remember and recall. The argument for this inability to track to the end of the model is that the marketplace presents too many intervening variables for an actual connection to be predicted between media advertising and sales. Consequently, current assumptions about "how media advertising works" generally only apply to the idea of transforming or changing attitudes held by consumers as a result of exposure to media advertising messages. This, then, leads to the vague notion that the attitude change (or reinforcement) will eventually impact consumer purchase behaviors on behalf of the advertised product or service.

This is an absurd fiction that benefits the augurs of conventional wisdom (Schultz & Pilotta, 2004). In fact, media that the consumer controls—such as TiVo, Internet surfing, researching of products, blogs and word-of-mouth—are not under the marketer's control anyway. The purchase funnel, based on the assumption of a hierarchy of effects model or approach, cannot and does not work with the new media forms. In truth, the sales-oriented purchase funnel is simply the hierarchy of effects turned on its side—these are two sides of the same coin. Given these challenges, the answer has to lie in more extensive consumer-centric research such as that provided by the SIMM data system.

Defining Media Engagement

In an attempt to maintain traditional media planning models and approaches currently in use, various media researchers and experts have suggested the importance of understanding media engagement—in other words, the assumption that consumers engage differently with various media forms. By adopting this concept, the hope is that the traditional outbound planning model, where distribution reigns supreme, can be retained. Engagement, pure and simple, is an act of communication. The term signifies a pledge or a promise. It requires a relationship in which two sides are brought together. Sending out messages, no matter how involving or exciting, does not create engagement; nor does the medium itself create value, if it is not consumed. Thus, while the concept of "engagement" is engaging, it has real problems when it is attempted in the marketplace.

In our mobile, multitasking society, engagement with media is generally intermittent; it is not sustained. It is also accompanied by background activity, such as listening to the radio or television, talking on the cell phone, reading the newspaper and being plugged into an MP3 player—all of this potentially occurring simultaneously. Thus, while engagement is an interesting concept, it really has little to do with how media planning can be improved or enhanced. That is all in the hands of the consumer—the person who consumes the media form and the content carried in that form and the ultimate decision maker as to whether or not to engage with the media form or the message.

Accountability

Consumer-centric media planning changes the face of media planning to address the demand for media accountability, in other words, the calculation or estimation of ROI. The methodologies used in many ROI estimates or calculations have typically neglected the front end of the process, that is, the planning and anticipation of sales based on verifiable purchase decisions. So, the allocation of media forms is predicated upon the expectation that they will result in positive returns to the advertiser. Negative ROI, regardless of the model employed, is a direct result of the weakness of front-end media planning models, since they commonly ignore or neglect the consumer. For example, current ROI models commonly assume that all humans have fixed tastes and expectations, attend to the same media forms and that one person's behavior has little or no effect on others. Clearly, all these are questionable assumptions but they make up the basis for much media planning.

The return on customer investment (ROCI) data collected in the BIGresearch system serves the growing need for such a consumer-oriented metric—one based upon consumer media consumption, not just upon marketer message and media distribution. Consumers clearly are not just passive receptacles of pleasure, or even of media entertainment. Instead, they appropriate and make investments of time, money, knowledge, information, trust and taste as key elements in their media consumption activities. This is the work that consumers do to participate in the interactive marketplace. Thus, consumers are also looking for a return on *their* investment from the retailers and manufacturers to enable them to most effectively allocate their most valuable asset, time, and to select which of the multitude of messages being directed toward them.

There are several key assumptions for a true consumer-centric model. First, customers must be viewed as assets. Second, the lifetime value (LTV) of the customer must equal the net present value (NPV) of the future customer. The classic ROI formula is as follows:

$$ROI = \frac{\text{NPV of incremental profits} - \text{NPV expenses}}{\text{NPV of expenses}}$$

There are, however, critics of the above formula. Some favor a direct NPV formula. Net present value is certainly better than ROI when ROI takes the rear-view mirror approach. NPV pretends to be a window on the future. However, it's merely a point in time just ahead of the rear-view mirror. It has little to do with what customers can or might do in the future.

The NPV is a financial metric that utilizes the Markov chain, which is a statistical term for an unconditional measure going into the future. That means it is a static model, which has to make assumptions about the future. It assumes that the future will be like the past. It cannot, however, identify the drivers of future expenditures and monitor those drivers monthly—a critical variable in media planning.

This issue revolves around the nature of the data used, the statistical tool employed and the assumptions the media planner makes. It is sufficient to say, future-oriented customer data that is conditional—what people say they intend to purchase going forward—takes those measures out of the static NPV mode and gives real-life possibilities for future customers, rather than made-up possibilities.

BIGresearch's consumer-centric data, as gathered through the SIMM system, is future oriented ; that is, what consumers anticipate or expect to do in the future. NPV, the discounted value of money received today versus in the future, is the critical component of an estimated ROI calculation. That makes the entire discussion meaningless although it continues to occur.

Return on Customer Investment

The return on customer investment (ROCI) model has been discussed in some detail by Schultz and Walters, who present it as a better way to measure the impact and effect of media advertising activities. It is based on the following key assumptions:

1. The customer is an asset.
2. The customer is a value creator.
3. Lifetime value should be based on NPV.

Additional elements in ROCI typically include channel performance, channel stock, market ratio of channel, macro-economic indicators, competing activity, economics, social concerns and media. These elements are better addressed by BIGresearch's orientation and data, which includes issues of ethnicity, as well as a variety of other variables than the traditional methodologies that simply assume these factors away.

BIGresearch's Consumer-Centric Elements for ROCI

BIGresearch regularly measures a number of variables that support the development of a sophisticated ROCI model.

For example, to better understand the consumer's point of view, BIGresearch, through the SIMM studies, captures information on thirty-one separate media forms which are designed to reflect the impact of media influence on purchase decisions, experiential time of media usage, daypart usage of media, simultaneous media usage, multitasking activities and media combinations, synergy by customer choice of media on purchase decisions and retail channel, likelihood of media allocation on success on purchases and in-store promotion. It is this type of consumer media usage and consumption that radically changes how media purchases can be planned, purchased and measured. Clearly, these are consumer measures, not media distribution measures which constitute the key element in the SIMM approach.

On the following pages, we identify the concepts, recommendations and expected outcomes possible through the use of the BIGresearch SIMM studies.

There is little question the media and purchasing consumption measures, using the new metrics founded on consumer-centric principles, are critical to marketing and advertising planning and management. The subject is all about changes and change and transformation. All key elements in today's very complex media marketplace.

References

Schultz, Don E. and Joseph J. Pilotta. "Developing the Foundation for a New Approach to Understanding How Media Advertising Works." 3rd ESOMAR/ARF World Audience Measurement Conference, June 13–18, 2005, Geneva.

Schultz, Don E., Joseph J. Pilotta and Martin P. Block. "Implementing a Media Consumption Model." 4th ESOMAR/ARF World Audience Measurement Conference, June 22–24, 2006, Montreal.

Schultz, Don E. and Jeffrey S. Walters. *Measuring Brand Communication ROI*. Association of National Advertisers, New York, 1997.

Wilbur Schramm and Donald F. Roberts, eds., *The Process and Effects of Mass Communication*. Urbana: University of Illinois Press, 1971.

Chapter

4

Media Generations

If, as has been argued in the first three chapters of this monograph, media consumption measures are radically different from media distribution measures, that raises the questions of: a) what is different and b) what new approaches might be employed to make use of the new consumption data coming from the SIMM studies.

One primary difference is in the current outbound, push-driven media planning system. In that approach, the marketer decides which media forms to employ, with what frequency and during what time periods. The primary tool media planners use to differentiate one medium from another and to make purchase decisions is through media distribution data using limited consumer information, usually demographics.

In the consumer-controlled pull system, it is the consumer who decides what medium will be selected from those available alternatives. The consumer does not have the same concerns as the marketer and, thus, uses a different media consumption calculus in making decisions.

For the most part, those decisions are driven by an internal cost-benefit analysis, which consumers have learned and internalized over time.

These internal media selection algorithms that consumers have developed over time—about media, media forms and media benefits—drive their media selections. In other words, they use personal experience to make most of their media decisions, although there are likely some external influences as well. Thus, we argue that over time, as they have experienced media and media forms, consumers have developed strong, internal media usage patterns. We believe these patterns have resulted in the development of what we call "media generations." Those are simply groups of people, who, having been exposed to certain types of media, have created groups and affiliations that they carry with them through their lives. Further, based on the SIMM data, we have been able to identify and measure those media generations. Thus, a new calculus for the media planner moves from traditional static measures, such as age, sex, income and lifestyle, to a totally new range of consumer behavioral measures—media generations.

In this chapter, we discuss this new concept and provide evidence of not only the existence of the various media generations we have identified, but also provide methods and ways in which this new information might be used in developing more effective media programs and schedules.

You Are What You Grew Up With

The media have traditionally used age as a way of describing their audiences, for example, adults 18–49 or teens or the over-65 group. These age groupings, while useful in terms of counting noses or pairs of eyeballs, are not very useful in the abstract. It is only when they are considered in the historical context in which these groups exist that they become worthwhile for planning and allocation approaches. The 25-year-old adult living today exists in a radically different world than a 25-year-old adult living in 1970, 1980 or even 1990.

At a minimum, media technology is different. In the 1970s, there were only three television networks; in the 1980s, cable was rapidly expanding viewing choices; and in the 1990s, the digital revolution was beginning. The political climate has changed, as have societal values. Fads have come and gone. Cultures have evolved. What was taboo only a few years ago is now de rigueur. So, age groups need to be put in their historical context, to be understood and relevant to media planners.

One way to do this is to consider the sociological concept of a generation. A generation has been traditionally defined as the interval of time between the birth of parents and their offspring. The typical span of time in the U.S. has been around 30 years. Arguably, it is getting longer as the median age of mothers continues to rise. However, considering a generation as a cohort of people born into and shaped by the events, trends and technology of their time, the time span should likely be shortened. For example, considering the current rate of technological change, ten years is a long time, and thirty years is almost a lifetime in terms of technology and changes in the overall environment.

Radio as an Example

Almost no one alive today in the U.S. can remember a time when there was no commercial radio. Radio throughout its history, with minor exceptions such as National Public Radio (NPR), has been an almost entirely advertiser-supported medium. As such, it has naturally linked itself to changing consumer tastes and preferences. Thus, the historical development of commercial radio provides special insights into the development of all media and marketing communication.

Radio faced a strong competitive threat in the mid-twentieth century from an emerging medium, television. That threat forced radio programming to move away from drama to music and talk in order to continue to attract and hold audiences.

Radio also has experienced dramatic changes in its own competitive structure with the introduction of Frequency Modulation (FM), and even technological change with FM stereo. Radio is also caught up in the digital age with the advent of Web and satellite radio.

Radio also has a retail component with the traditional remote broadcast and growing in-store radio activities. It also has the advantage of both local and national advertising rates.

Much can be learned about how consumers take in, accept and use radio from an examination of radio formats. In the 1930s, radio was dominated by dramatic productions and serials such as *The Thin Man, Boston Blackie* and the like. Those were followed by comedies such as *Amos 'n' Andy*, and dramas such as *Gunsmoke*—and even variety programs such as *Arthur Godfrey's Talent Scouts*. These formats either migrated to television or ceased production as radio morphed into a more individualized media form.

Early 1950s radio was dominated by 'middle-of-the-road' (MOR) programming, which consisted of both talk and music. Country music was beginning to attract an audience, but it wasn't until rock and roll and the Top 40 format appeared that things began to change.

In the 1960s, partly because of the introduction of FM, differing radio formats began to proliferate. The timeline of contemporary music formats (Figure 7) illustrates how quickly those changes developed. Not only was the audience fragmenting, as increasingly narrow new formats emerged, but the first 'oldie' format appeared. By the time 1990s arrived, oldie formats existed across multiple time spans, including the 1970s and 1980s.

From the SIMM data, it appears the old radio adage that: "you listen to the music that was popular when you were growing up" is true. Those that were teens in the 1960s, continue to listen to the same rock and roll formats and artists throughout the rest of their lives. Simply go to any Kiss or Rolling Stones concert and verify how audiences remain loyal to their earlier idols.

This leads to the concept of media generations. Consumers of different age cohorts use media in the way they did while they were growing up. The radio age generation or cohort concept, can, we believe, be applied to all forms of media and marketing communication. The problem then becomes one of defining the age cohorts.

FIGURE 7: TIMELINE OF CONTEMPORARY MUSIC FORMATS

Source: RemergeMedia.com

Using the American Generation Typology

Strauss and Howe in their book *Generations*, published in 1991, tell the history of America as a succession of generational biographies from the colonial period through the present. The authors identify a pattern in each of these generations. Each can be seen as belonging to one of four archetypes that repeat sequentially. Every living generation, therefore, shows a remarkable parallel in character with generations of the same type throughout history. The book plots a recurring cycle of spiritual awakenings and secular crises in American history—from the founding colonials through the present day.

In 1997, Strauss and Howe published *The Fourth Turning*, which expanded on *Generations*. The book proposes that modern history moves in cycles, each one lasting approximately the length of a long human life (about 80-years), and each composed of four eras, or "turnings." Analyzing primarily the period from the end of World War II until today, they describe the general persona of each living generation—from the thoughtful Silent Generation (born before 1945), to the values-obsessed Baby Boomers (born between 1946 and 1964), and on to the pragmatic Thirteenth Generation (the thirteenth since the U.S. became a nation, born 1965 to 1980 or so), to the newest proactive Millennial Generation (born after 1980). According to Strauss and Howe, the Millennials could emerge as the next great generation.

American Generational Archetypes

Strauss and Howe expand their interpretation of the generations by giving them archetypical names. The generations come in four different archetypes: Prophet, Nomad, Hero and Artist.

Prophets are values-driven, moralistic, focused on self and willing to fight for what they believe. They grow up as increasingly indulged children, come of age as the young crusaders, enter midlife as moralistic leaders and enter elderhood as wise leaders. The Boomers are an example of a Prophet generation.

Nomads are diverse, adventurous and cynical about institutions. They grow up as the as protected children, come of age as alienated young adults, become pragmatic midlife leaders and enter elderhood as tough elders. The Thirteenth Generation (Generation X) and the Lost Generation are examples of Nomad generations.

Heroes are conventional, powerful and institutionally driven, with a profound trust in authority. They grow up as protected children, come of age as team-working units, become energetic and hubristic midlifers and become powerful elders. The G.I. Generation that fought World War II is an example of a Hero generation. Millennials are expected to emerge as the next generation of this example.

Artists are subtle, indecisive, emotional and compromising. They grow up as the over-protected children, come of age as the sensitive young adults, rebel as indecisive midlife leaders and become empathic elders. The Silent Generation is an example of an Artist generation.

FIGURE 8: RECENT GENERATIONS AND THEIR ARCHETYPES

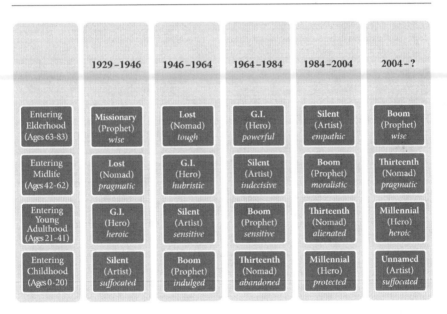

	1929–1946	1946–1964	1964–1984	1984–2004	2004–?
Entering Elderhood (Ages 63-83)	Missionary (Prophet) *wise*	Lost (Nomad) *tough*	G.I. (Hero) *powerful*	Silent (Artist) *empathic*	Boom (Prophet) *wise*
Entering Midlife (Ages 42-62)	Lost (Nomad) *pragmatic*	G.I. (Hero) *hubristic*	Silent (Artist) *indecisive*	Boom (Prophet) *moralistic*	Thirteenth (Nomad) *pragmatic*
Entering Young Adulthood (Ages 21-41)	G.I. (Hero) *heroic*	Silent (Artist) *sensitive*	Boom (Prophet) *sensitive*	Thirteenth (Nomad) *alienated*	Millennial (Hero) *heroic*
Entering Childhood (Ages 0-20)	Silent (Artist) *suffocated*	Boom (Prophet) *indulged*	Thirteenth (Nomad) *abandoned*	Millennial (Hero) *protected*	Unnamed (Artist) *suffocated*

Source: Strauss and Howe, *The Fourth Turning*, page 83.

Strauss and Howe believe that history shapes each generation depending on what phase of life it occupies as it encounters key historical events. For example, a period of crisis will leave an impression on children that will be different from the one it leaves on midlife leaders. The boundaries of each generation and the characteristics of its members emerge because they share a common age and location in history. For instance, Strauss and Howe define the Boomer generation as anyone who doesn't personally remember World War II. They are different from the Silent Generation because they have not shared the experience of childhood during a war. Thus, history creates the generations, and these in turn reproduce the cycle of history. As the protected children of a time without a crisis, such as World War II, they become moralistic, uncompromising crusaders as they age, and are most likely to provoke a new crisis when they grow to control the nation's institutions. That pattern is shown in Figure 8.

The critical idea is that the experiences of childhood, especially the teenage years, impact the shape and the course of later life. This, we argue, is true of media usage and, thus, media consumption as well. That is, the way media and marketing communication are learned during childhood determines the patterns for the rest of one's life, even though new media and technologies appear. As will be seen in the SIMM data to follow, Boomers use the Internet, but they use it differently than do the Millennials who grew up with it.

The generations have been named and renamed by various authors over recent years. Multiple names are more common among the more recent generations. There is also some minor disagreement on when the various generations start and end. We use the following as the format for this text.

The Silent Generation, born between the two World Wars (1925–1945), is the one with most agreement. Members of this generation are now in their mid-sixties or older. The Baby Boomers, born between 1946 and 1964, are the generation born after World War II, and represent the increased worldwide birth rate that occurred during that period. Baby Boomers, now in their mid-forties to early sixties, were in their teen and college years during the 1960s, with its counter culture and the Vietnam war. The Boomers gave birth to what have become known as Generations X and Y.

The leading edge of the Thirteenth Generation is also referred to as Generation Jones, or sometimes Tweeners since they were born between the Boomers and Generation X. While the trailing edge is commonly referred to as Generation X. This term was first popularized in a novel by Douglas Coupland, *Generation X: Tales for an Accelerated Culture* (1991). Generation X is sometimes also referred to as Baby Busters. Most of this generation are children of Boomers and Silents. They grew up with video games, MTV and the end of the Cold War. They are now in their thirties and forties.

Whereas, the XY Cusp, the MTV Generation or the Boomerang Generation (born between 1975 and 1986), are now mostly in their late twenties. And Generation Y (Echo Boom, Internet Generation or Millennials) were born after 1980, although there is disagreement on the exact date. This generation is mostly in their twenties and late teens and grew up with the Internet. Sometimes, the younger portion of this group is referred to as Generation I, since the Internet has become such a part of their lives.

U.S. Media Generations

The generations described above can be matched to different styles of media consumption and usage, even though the media environment has changed and evolved across the media generations. For example, the Leading Baby Boomer Generation (born 1946–56) grew up during the expansion of over-the-air broadcast television and the traditional three networks. The most popular magazines were high circulation general interest publications such as *Life*, *Look* and *The Saturday Evening Post*. Radio was dominated by middle-of-the-road talk radio when the leading Boomers were children. Thus, it is easy to name this generation the Mass (Media) Generation.

Following the Mass Generation are the Trailing Boomers, that is, the children (born 1957–64) who grew up following Sputnik and the space race. A good media name for this generation might be the Space Generation. Their common experience is the proliferation of media choices with FM radio, more magazine titles and the growth of cable television. Figure 9 shows a summary of the media generations we have created from the SIMM data.

Next is the Hippie Generation. These are the children (born 1965–74) that grew up during the counter-culture movement and the Vietnam War—the leading edge of Strauss and Howe's Thirteenth Generation, or Generation Jones.

The trailing edge of the Thirteenth Generation (born 1975–87) is Generation X and its characteristic, in media terms, was the introduction and early acceptance of the personal computer. Thus, we have named this group the Computer Generation. Computer communication, at least during the time this generation were children, was limited to proprietary networks such as Prodigy and CompuServe.

The last, and youngest generation, generally referred to as Millennials (born from 1988 onwards), grew up with the Internet. It's easy to name this group the Internet Generation.

Figure 10 shows some historical highlights for each of the most recent media generations. The Mass Generation saw the advent of network television and the very beginnings of color broadcasting and cable television. The Space Generation saw satellite communication for the first time. The Hippie Generation had Woodstock and proliferating media forms. The Computer Generation has been dominated by the growth of the personal computer and computing. The Internet Generation has seen the digital revolution and the beginnings and acceptance of social networking media.

FIGURE 9: U.S. Generation Summary

Media Generation	Traditional Names	Other Names	Birth Years	Notable Events
Silent Generation	Silent Generation		1925-1945	WWII
Mass Generation	Leading Baby Boomers	Boomers	1946-1956	Start of Cold War
Space Generation	Trailing Baby Boomers	Beat Generation	1957-1964	Space Race
Hippie Generation	Thirteenth Generation	Generation Jones	1965-1974	Vietnam War
Computer Generation	Thirteenth Generation	Generation X	1975-1987	End of Cold War/ War on Terror
Internet Generation	Millennial Generation	Generation Y	1988-	Digital Globalization

FIGURE 10: U.S. Media History and Generations

Mass Generation (Leading Boomers)	Space Generation (Trailing Boomers)	Hippie Generation (Generation Jones)	Computer Generation (Generation X)	Internet Generation (Millennial)
1940: The first commercial television station signs on the air.	1957: Soviet Union's Sputnik is launched.	1965: Vietnam War becomes the first war to be televised.	1975: Home version of *Pong* from Atari is available.	1991: Internet is made available for commercial use.
1948: Cable Television becomes available.	1958: First U.S. satellite, Explorer I, is launched.	1966: In China, the Cultural Revolution takes place.	1975: HBO bounces signal off satellite to reach cable systems and customers.	1991: Soviet anti-Gorbachev plot collapses, aided by the Internet.

Mass Generation	Space Generation	Hippie Generation	Computer Generation	Internet Generation
1950: Nielsen's Audimeter tracks television audiences.	1960: *Tiros I* is the first weather satellite.	1969: Astronauts send live photos from the Moon.	1975: Bill Gates and Paul Allen start Microsoft.	1995: Direct Broadcast Satellites are launched.
1951: Color television sets go on sale.	1961: FM stereo broadcasting begins.	1969: The Woodstock music festival takes place.	1976: Small satellite dishes are set up in residential backyards.	1998: HDTV broadcasts begin in the United States.
1952: Atomic bomb test in Nevada shows on live television.	1962: Cable companies import distant signals.	1970: FM stations target population segments.	1981: The laptop computer is launched.	2001: Satellite radio; XM begins broadcasting.
1953: CATV system uses microwave to bring in distant signals.	1962: John Glenn's earth orbit is televised.	1971: E-mail starts.	1981: The IBM PC is released.	2001: Instant messaging, or short messaging service (SMS), grows in popularity.
1955: President Eisenhower's news conference is televised.	1963: The Beatles shake up music.	1972: Videocassette movies are for sale or rent in stores.	1983: Japan's NHK presents HDTV.	2001: The iPod music player is released.

Mass Generation	Space Generation	Hippie Generation	Computer Generation	Internet Generation
	1963: Communications satellite is launched.	1972: HBO starts pay-TV service for cable.	1983: AT&T is forced to break up; 7 Baby Bells are born.	2003: MySpace.com starts.
	1963: Martin Luther King gives "I have a dream" speech.	1974: President Nixon resigns; 110 million viewers watch.	1986: A fourth U.S. television network, Fox, is added to the ABC, CBS, NBC lineup.	2004: "Podcasting" is coined as a term for Internet delivery of radio-style content.

Chinese Media Generations

To this point, we have discussed only U.S. media generations. BIGresearch is gathering similar SIMM-type data in China. This gives an initial perspective on how media consumption and, thus, media generations have developed in other countries and other cultures. We discuss the preliminary Chinese data now simply to illustrate the point of cultural differences in the media generations and the various countries and cultures.

We use only the two most recent China Quarterly data sets to discuss the overall concept.

Historically, China has experienced different events from the U.S. One of the key events was the Cultural Revolution. Therefore, we separate the data into the Chinese Pre-Cultural Revolution and Post-Cultural Revolution Generations. This division corresponds fairly closely to the U.S. Boomer and Thirteenth Generation boundary.

In China, those that follow are referred to as Generation X (as in the U.S.). This roughly matches what we have termed the Computer Generation for the U.S. The youngest generation, Millennials, are perhaps the most similar to the U.S. generation of the same name. This generation can no doubt also be referred to as the Internet Generation in both the U.S. and China.

In other monographs and reports, we will detail the development of the Chinese media generations and how those might be considered. For now, we believe it is clear that the media generations and, thus, media usage vary by country and by the form of media consumers use. Thus, we return to the discussion of the U.S. media generations.

FIGURE 11: CHINESE GENERATIONS

Name	Birth Years
Red Generation	1925-1950
Pre-Cultural Revolution	1951-1964
Post-Cultural Revolution	1965-1973
Generation X	1974-1984
Millennial	1985-

U.S. Media Generation Characteristics

Consumption of the various radio formats, based on BIGresearch SIMM study results for the first half of 2008 (see Figure 12) vary predictably by media generation. The Silent Generation prefers oldies, country, talk, news and classical. Form and format preferences begin to change among the Mass Generation, notably, the preference for oldies becomes much more pronounced. The Space and Hippie generations begin to prefer rock. The Hippie Generation expands their repertoire from just Top 40 to include pop. The youngest generations, Computer and Internet, continue with their preference for rock, but also add hip-hop and alternative radio formats.

FIGURE 12: RADIO FORMATS LISTENED TO BY MEDIA GENERATION *(The numbers in the table are percentages.)*

	Silent	Mass	Space	Hippie	Computer	Internet	Total
Rock	10	28	43	43	46	45	37
Oldies	41	50	34	20	19	16	32
Country	32	28	27	26	24	18	26
Top 40/Pop	6	16	29	35	35	30	26
R&B	8	16	20	23	33	30	22
Talk	34	25	23	21	14	9	21
Hip-Hop	1	4	10	22	39	41	19
News	31	22	19	17	13	10	19
Alternative	3	7	15	21	32	31	18
Classical	23	17	12	10	11	11	14
Jazz	15	17	16	11	10	9	14
Religious	14	16	18	15	11	12	14
Sports	14	12	12	13	13	10	13

Source: BIGresearch

Demographically, the media segments show differences beyond just age. The highest incomes, as shown in Figure 13, are enjoyed by the Mass, Space and Hippie generations, with an average household income at about $60,000. Income drops among the younger segments, as might be expected. Owning a home and being married both increase with age. Presence of children in the household under the age of 18 decreases among the Silent and Mass Generation, as would be expected. The proportion is still high, however, among the Internet Generation as they are likely still living at home with siblings. The Silent Generation has the highest proportion of retired people, while the Internet Generation has the highest proportion of students. Professional occupations appear to be highest among the Hippie Generation. There are the most clerical workers among the Space and Hippie generations. Unemployment seems, as is typically the case, to be the highest among the younger generations.

FIGURE 13: SELECT DEMOGRAPHICS BY MEDIA GENERATIONS *(The numbers in the table are percentages.)*

	Silent	Mass	Space	Hippie	Computer	Internet	Total
Income (000)	53.8	61.8	61.0	59.9	44.8	38.7	55.0
Own Home	83.8	75.8	69.9	63.4	33.8	19.6	60.1
Under 18 Present	5.6	13.9	41.1	60.8	41.1	44.5	34.2
Married	63.2	60.8	58.5	56.4	31.6	3.5	49.7
College Grad +	40.5	35.9	31.9	37.2	33.4	1.6	33.6
Occupation:							
Business Owner	5.9	8.3	8.0	6.6	3.9	0.8	6.2
Professional	10.4	30.1	36.5	38.1	24.2	1.8	27.6
Salesperson	1.4	3.0	2.4	2.6	5.3	4.9	3.3
Laborer	0.8	3.3	4.4	4.0	4.3	2.1	3.5
Clerical Worker	3.0	10.3	13.9	13.9	10.5	3.9	10.5
Homemaker	3.6	5.3	6.8	9.4	7.5	1.6	6.5
Student	0.1	0.4	0.5	0.9	14.5	50.9	6.5
Retired	62.8	14.9	1.6	0.3	0.1	0.0	10.8
Unemployed	0.5	2.9	3.4	3.1	7.6	10.7	4.3

Source: BIGresearch

It is interesting that there is an array of interests and activities that are preferred at approximately the same level for all generations. Figure 14 shows the top ten similar activities, which include watching television, eating meals out, reading books, magazines and newspapers, travel and cooking.

FIGURE 14: ACTIVITIES WITH THE SMALLEST DIFFERENCES BY MEDIA GENERATIONS (*The numbers in the table are percentages.*)

	Silent	Mass	Space	Hippie	Computer	Internet	Total
Watch TV	72	75	73	75	77	76	75
Eating Out	66	68	70	72	74	69	70
Listen to Music	51	60	63	66	72	81	65
Read Books	60	62	61	60	56	56	59
Mags/News	54	53	52	50	49	43	51
Travel	52	52	49	50	50	40	50
Cooking	34	40	45	43	42	35	41
Camp/Fish	24	29	32	33	37	32	32
Any Hobby	22	23	24	22	24	24	23
Golf	15	12	11	12	14	12	13

Source: BIGresearch

Figure 15 shows the top ten most dissimilar activities, or the activities that vary the most across segments. These may well explain why the observed differences between the media generations occur. Among the most different are the incidences of movies, e-mail, IM (instant messaging) and blogs, video games, active sports including team sports, swimming, tennis and gardening.

FIGURE 15: ACTIVITIES WITH THE GREATEST DIFFERENCES BY MEDIA GENERATIONS *(The numbers in the table are percentages.)*

	Silent	Mass	Space	Hippie	Computer	Internet	Total
Go to Movies	30	45	54	62	72	77	56
Rent Videos	18	30	39	46	55	54	41
E-mail/IM/Blogging	35	31	33	40	55	66	41
Amusement Parks	9	21	32	45	49	52	34
Gardening	38	40	39	31	20	12	31
Play Video Games	8	14	20	33	50	62	29
Swimming	16	19	27	31	39	42	28
Go to Night Club	5	11	17	23	45	24	23
Play Team Sports	2	4	8	14	27	36	14
Tennis	3	4	6	8	13	17	8

Source: BIGresearch

Figure 16 shows the activities and interests that are associated with each media generation. Watching TV, for example, is the most commonly selected activity for every generation with the exception of the Internet group, the youngest in the sample. If we compare the average interest across all the items in the BIGresearch SIMM data, some thought-provoking insights begin to appear. Between the Silent and Hippie generations the average percent drops from about 37% to a low of 27%. Both the Computer and Internet generations are more interested in more things with averages at 40% or a little higher.

FIGURE 16: Top Activity Interests and Average
Interest Level by Media Generations
(*The numbers in the table are percentages.*)

Silent	Mass	Space	Hippie	Computer	Internet
Watch TV	Watch TV	Watch TV	Watch TV	Watch TV	Music
Eating Out	Eating Out	Eating Out	Eating Out	Eating Out	Surf Internet
Read Books	Read Books	Music	Listen to Music	Surf Internet	Go to Movies
Mags/News	Music	Read Books	Surf Internet	Listen to Music	Watch TV
Travel	Surf Internet	Surf Internet	Go to Movies	Go to Movies	Eating Out
Music	Mags/News	Go to Movies	Read Books	Go Shopping	E-mail/IM
Surf Internet	Travel	Mags/News	Family Activities	Read Books	Video Games
Socializing	Go to Movies	Travel	Go Shopping	Rent Videos	Socializing
Gardening	Go Shopping	Go Shopping	Mags/News	E-mail/IM	Read Books
E-mail/IM	Cooking	Family	Travel	Socializing	Rent Videos
27.3	31.0	33.9	36.6	41.2	40.0

Source: BIGresearch

Figure 17 shows health conditions by media generation. The Silent Generation has the most health conditions, especially arthritis, high blood pressure and high cholesterol. The younger segments have more allergies, depression and insomnia.

FIGURE 17: HEALTH BY MEDIA GENERATIONS

(*The numbers in the table are percentages.*)

	Silent	Mass	Space	Hippie	Computer	Internet	Total
Allergies	27	34	39	40	39	37	36
Overweight	31	37	35	34	24	17	31
High BP	49	38	24	13	7	4	23
Headaches	5	13	21	23	26	24	19
High Cholesterol	38	31	20	11	6	3	19
Arthritis	35	28	19	9	5	4	17
Acid Reflux	19	20	19	15	12	9	16
Insomnia	9	14	19	14	16	16	15
Depression	8	12	15	14	18	17	14
Heartburn	11	14	16	13	12	8	13
Diabetes	20	16	10	5	4	2	10
Heart Disease	11	6	3	1	1	1	4

Source: BIGresearch

Selected purchase behavior, shown in Figure 18, indicates high levels of online purchasing for all segments, although the Internet Generation reports a higher level of "occasionally purchase online" compared with the others. Younger segments are more likely to purchase organic products, and the Hippie and Computer generations are most likely to purchase beer, wine or other types of alcohol. Fast food restaurant visits are highest among the Hippie Generation.

FIGURE 18: PURCHASE BEHAVIOR BY MEDIA GENERATIONS
(*The numbers in the table are percentages.*)

	Silent	Mass	Space	Hippie	Computer	Internet	Total
Purchase Online:							
Regularly	21.8	27.2	29.2	29.8	27.9	15.9	27.1
Occasionally	67.0	64.3	62.8	64.0	64.3	71.1	64.6
Never	11.1	8.5	8.0	6.2	7.8	12.9	8.3
Purchase Alcohol	68.1	71.7	78.8	79.8	83.1	64.9	76.5
Purchase Organics	64.3	66.9	68.8	68.7	72.7	75.0	69.1
Eat Fast Food (Month)	3.7	4.4	4.8	5.2	4.8	4.4	4.6
Credit Cards:							
Visa	71	67	64	64	56	37	62
Master Card	62	57	51	52	38	18	49
Store Credit Card	32	30	27	22	16	5	23
Discover Card	34	29	24	19	14	4	22
American Express	24	19	16	14	10	4	15

Source: BIGresearch

Figure 19 shows that the younger segments are the ones buying and driving foreign cars. It is also interesting that both Computer and Internet generations report being more likely not to own a car. Figure 20 shows the Internet and Computer generations to be far more likely to download music or videos to an iPod or cell phone than are other groups. Yet, it seems that all generations do participate in downloading music.

FIGURE 19: CAR OWNERSHIP BY MEDIA GENERATION
(*The numbers in the table are percentages.*)

	Silent	Mass	Space	Hippie	Computer	Internet	Total
Do not own	2.5	2.9	3.3	3.5	6.9	14.6	4.5
Toyota	11.1	10.3	9.2	9.0	10.3	8.6	9.9
Honda	8.0	6.8	8.5	9.3	9.0	7.7	8.2
Nissan	3.3	4.1	4.5	5.3	6.2	4.9	4.8
Other Foreign	15.1	17.0	16.9	17.8	18.8	20.8	17.5
Total Foreign	37.5	38.2	39.0	41.5	44.3	42.0	40.5
Ford	13.1	13.6	16.5	13.4	11.6	12.6	13.5
Chevrolet	10.6	13.6	13.9	12.7	11.9	10.0	12.6
Pontiac	2.3	3.0	2.8	3.4	4.2	3.3	3.2
Dodge	5.1	7.3	5.4	7.7	5.6	4.4	6.2
Chrysler	4.1	4.6	4.3	3.6	2.4	2.7	3.7
Jeep	2.7	2.7	2.8	3.4	3.8	1.5	3.1
Other Domestic	22.0	14.3	12.0	10.8	9.1	8.9	12.7
Total Domestic	60.0	58.9	57.7	55.0	48.8	43.4	55.1

Source: BIGresearch

FIGURE 20: DEVICE DOWNLOADED TO BY MEDIA
GENERATION (*The numbers in the table are percentages.*)

	Silent	Mass	Space	Hippie	Computer	Internet	Total
PC	34.0	35.8	38.1	45.1	54.1	54.8	43.2
iPod	4.3	11.2	18.0	28.6	33.5	41.4	21.8
MP3 Player	3.4	7.4	12.1	19.5	23.0	29.1	14.9
Cell Phone	2.5	6.3	9.7	17.0	24.9	28.9	14.1
Mac	2.9	2.7	2.7	3.2	6.8	8.2	4.1

Source: BIGresearch

The SIMM data clearly shows that media generations do exist in the U.S. population and can be identified based on the media forms they consume. Further, the SIMM data helps in understanding the types of products the generations consume and, thus, provides potential for predictive valuation going forward. The value of this data is that it provides media planners and buyers new ways to consider audiences when allocating media resources. It is another step in truly building customer-centric media plans.

In Chapter 5, we begin to tie the various views of consumers together by understanding media usage and media influence on purchases.

References

Dou, Wenyu, Guangping Wang and Nan Zhou. "Generational and Regional Differences in Media Consumption Patterns of Chinese Generation X Consumers." *Journal of Advertising* 35 (Summer 2006) 101-110.

Strauss, William and Neil Howe. *The Fourth Turning*. Broadway Books, New York, 1998.

Strauss, William and Neil Howe. *Generations*. William Morrow, New York, 1991.

Chapter

5

Media Usage

When we start from a consumer view of media, as illustrated in the media generations approach discussed in the last chapter, different media measures are clearly needed. Historically, media have been measured based on their distribution, not on their consumption. Even the most sophisticated media measurement systems of today don't measure consumer consumption of the media form, they measure only exposure or opportunities to see (OTS). Thus, to move to a consumer-oriented consumption model of media allocation and measurement, we must develop new approaches and methodologies. That has been done, using the SIMM data. We discuss this in more detail in this chapter.

To understand the radically different view consumer media consumption brings to the media planning and allocation area, we start first with a review of the current state-of-the-art in media measurement for it is the way media is measured that drive how it is allocated.

Media Measurement Today

Media have traditionally been measured on the basis of their distribution, with consumption added, where possible, as an attempt to demonstrate the medium's value. Most measures are attempts to illustrate consumer choice in a particular media category, for example, Channel 5 vs. Channel 7 or National Geographic vs. Atlantic. This typically has been referred to as intra-media comparison.

In all cases, as above, current day measures involve primarily OTS or potential exposure. For example, if a magazine or newspaper is delivered to a home, the assumption is made that it was consumed (read) by some people for some period of time. Broadcast media is measured in the same way—if the set is on, it is assumed that someone is watching or listening. In other words, what is being measured is "opportunity to consume" not actual consumption.

Broadcast media have typically been measured according to their rating points (the percent of households viewing or listening, compared with the total market) within a specific time period (usually a quarter hour) or daypart. Thus, the idea is that Station A can be directly compared with station B in terms of the potential audience it delivers in the specified time period. This is generally aggregated to longer time periods, such as a week, in the form of gross rating points (the sum of the ratings) for the time period. The ratings can be easily translated into an OTS audience, either as a net unduplicated audience or reach, or as a duplicated or gross audience. The reach is generally divided into the gross audience to estimate average frequency (see Chapter 3).

The print media audience is typically measured in terms of the households receiving the publication or the persons claiming to read it. Claiming to read has a number of measurement advantages, but, for the most part, they are designed to show, again, that one publication has a larger audience (more people reading) than another publication. Because print media measures are quite different from broadcast media, it is difficult to directly compare them. A classic argument has been over the value of an exposure to a thirty-second television commercial compared with seeing a full-page advertisement in a magazine.

Time Allocation as a New Media Measure

Given the difficulties of determining who is reading, watching or listening, one way to make the media usage standard across all media categories is to measure the time spent with it by individuals, not by households exposed. Media usage, thus, becomes a time allocation problem. The premise is simple: consumers would allocate more time to media that are more attractive or of greater interest or provide greater value to them as individuals. Those media that have fewer consumer values would be allocated less time by those same individuals. Thus, reported time spent with each of the 31 media forms tracked in the SIMM studies becomes one of the key ingredients in understanding media consumption.

Time budget studies have long been used to determine lifestyles and to make group comparisons, such as working and non-working women, or across different countries or regions. Media consumption, as reported by the audience, then, can be expressed as an average number of minutes per day. Keeping in mind that there are 1440 minutes in a day (24 hours x 60 minutes per hour) the average could also be expressed as a percentage of the day. For example, if someone sleeps for 8 hours, that converts to 480 minutes, or 33% of the day.

Measuring media consumption in minutes provides a uniform basis of comparison across all media categories. Obviously, media consumption changes across time periods. For example, weekdays are different from weekends, which allow for more discretionary media time. However, to keep the analysis simple, in the SIMM reports that follow weekdays are averaged together with weekends.

There is also the problem of simultaneous media consumption, that is, a person consuming two or more media at the same time. We will ignore that issue for the moment, but return to it later, as it is a key element in media consumption.

The media categories included here are those that are measured through the BIGresearch SIMM studies.

Media Consumption

The most obvious question that arises is, are all media consumed in the same way? The answer, of course, is no—but, not always for the reasons that are commonly thought. We now look at individual media forms and discuss what we have learned from the SIMM data over the past six years.

Television

Television has historically been considered the dominant mass medium in the United States. As we will show in this section, a major argument about the level of that dominance can be made today.

On average, the typical American spent 129.6 minutes per day watching TV, a little over two hours, during the first half of 2008. This based on the reports of a sample of 17,327 consumers who make up a representative sample of the entire U.S. population.

Figure 21 shows the individual media usage trend, based on SIMM data, over the past three years, or six SIMM reporting periods. The period-to-period changes indicate some volatility in usage, moving from a high of 137.1 minutes in December 2006 to a low of 126.7 minutes in December 2005. Overall television usage in the U.S. is increasing slightly, that is, at an average rate of 0.6% over the six SIMM data periods reported here. This has occurred despite the decline in consumption in the most recent period.

There is disagreement over the amount of time consumers spend with television. Figure 22 shows the estimates of several sources for June 2005. This is the last time all of the measures could be compared at the same point in time. The BIGresearch estimate of 145.6 minutes for June 2005 is considerably higher than that shown for December 2005 in Figure 21. As shown, there was a substantial drop in 2005.

FIGURE 21: TV Usage Trend (in Minutes)

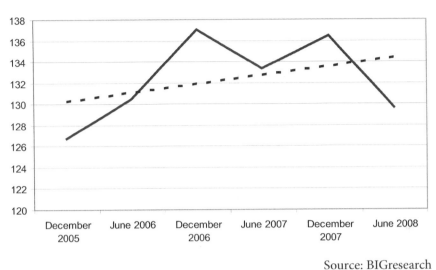

Source: BIGresearch

FIGURE 22: U.S. Average TV Usage (Estimates for June 2005)

	Minutes per Day
BIGresearch	145.6
Online self-reported recall (n=15,000)	
American Time Use Survey*	154.8
Time budget interview (n=13,000)	
ACNielsen	259.2
People Meter (n=5,000)	
Middletown II**	266.0
Observation (n=300)	

Source: BIGresearch

* Ball State University
** U.S. Bureau of Labor Statistics

The BIGresearch estimate is reasonably close to that of the U.S. Bureau of Labor Statistics American Time Use Survey, which is 155 minutes. The estimate, however, is considerably below the Nielsen estimate of nearly 260 minutes. This can be partly explained since Nielsen estimate of over four hours per day is for a household, whereas the BIGresearch estimate is for an individual. There are also some possible methodological biases inherent in the two measures, which we will not discuss at this point.

Media Usage by Media Generation

The figures above are all aggregated audiences. While that information is useful for the media planner, the more important question is, "who are the people who are doing the watching," or "who are the media consumers and what do we know about them"? It is this granularity that becomes critical when selecting one media form over the other or one media vehicle over the other. The following data, which helps the media planner in understanding these issues, comes from the SIMM studies using the concept of media generations.

The Silent Generation reports watching the most television, about 136 minutes per day, as shown in Figure 23. The Hippie Generation reports watching the least, at 125 minutes, which is only an 11-minute difference. The Internet Generation also watches less television, at 126 minutes. In general, it is probably safe to assume that television watching increases with age, which has major implications for media planning and buying, particularly when only household data is available to the marketer.

Differences are greater among the types of television programs consumed (reported watched) than the average minutes per day. This intra-media comparison is a key element in most media plans. Figure 24 shows some of the seemingly age-related skews observed.

FIGURE 23: TELEVISION CONSUMPTION BY MEDIA
GENERATIONS (JUNE 2008)

	Minutes per Day
Silent	136.1
Mass	132.3
Space	130.5
Hippie	124.6
Computer	130.3
Internet	126.0
Total	129.6

Source: BIGresearch

FIGURE 24: TV PROGRAMMING PREFERENCES BY MEDIA
GENERATION (JUNE 2008)

	Silent	Mass	Space	Hippie	Computer	Internet	Total
Movies	41	46	46	45	46	42	45
Drama shows	37	41	41	38	35	28	38
Police/detective shows	39	40	38	36	32	24	36
Situation comedy	25	32	34	35	32	29	32
Documentaries	33	33	31	30	27	22	30
Sports	33	31	31	30	28	24	30
Cooking	22	27	29	28	25	19	26
Reality TV	14	20	26	29	31	27	25
Home improvement	24	29	29	27	20	13	25
Game shows	25	23	22	21	23	22	23
Talk shows	24	23	23	21	20	18	22
Cartoons	7	12	17	25	30	29	20
Music video	6	9	15	18	24	26	16
NASCAR	12	12	12	11	10	8	11
Soap operas	7	9	12	12	12	10	11
Religious shows	11	10	11	10	8	7	10
Wrestling	3	4	5	8	10	10	7

Source: BIGresearch

Clearly, if the media planner uses the media generations concept, some new insights and implications arise in terms of how media might be allocated. By a considerable margin, movies are the media content that is most widely consumed by all generations. Music videos are highly skewed toward the younger groups, as are reality shows. Thus, with the SIMM data, the planner can go beyond the basic demographics as reported by the syndicated audience measurement companies.

Radio

Radio measures have become quite complicated as a result of the addition of satellite and Web radio to the spectrum choices. Figure 25 shows the total radio consumption at 129.9 minutes a day. This shows that virtually the same amount of time was spent with radio in the U.S. in June 2008 as was spent with television. This is composed of 93.5 minutes of terrestrial radio, 22.0 minutes of satellite radio, and 14.4 minutes of Web radio.

FIGURE 25: Radio Usage by Type (in Minutes)

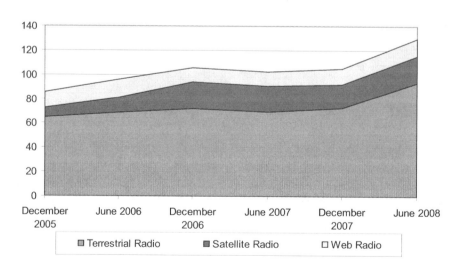

Source: BIGresearch

As Figure 26 shows, consumption of radio as a medium is grow-ing—at the average rate of 1.4% for the half-year period of this SIMM data. That is almost twice the growth rate of television viewing. The growth pattern of radio has been reasonably consistent during the time of the SIMM studies.

FIGURE 26: ALL RADIO USAGE TREND (IN MINUTES)

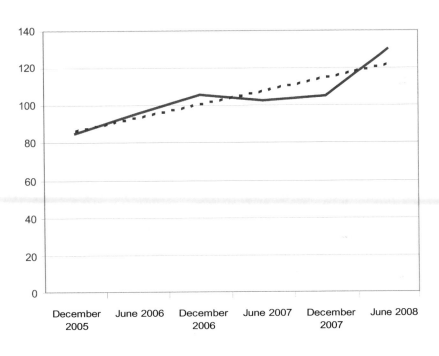

Source: BIGresearch

As might be expected, there are major variations in how the vari-ous forms of radio are consumed. Figure 27 shows radio consumption by media generations. Clearly, the new forms of radio broadcast are unevenly distributed with satellite appealing to the older groups and web radio to the younger.

FIGURE 27: RADIO CONSUMPTION BY MEDIA GENERATIONS
(JUNE 2008)

	Terrestrial	Satellite	Web	All Radio
Silent	78.0	20.2	4.6	102.8
Mass	91.7	20.9	7.8	120.4
Space	100.2	21.3	11.8	133.3
Hippie	99.2	25.8	16.8	141.8
Computer	95.3	22.5	23.3	141.0
Internet	80.1	19.0	23.9	122.8
Total	93.3	22.0	14.4	129.9

Source: BIGresearch

Internet

The Internet consists of a variety of marketing communication activities including banner ads, pop-ups and Web sites. These are the media forms that are most often included when search and keyword marketing are considered. Figure 28 shows that an average of 127.5 minutes per day was spent by consumers in June 2008 on Internet and Internet-related activities. Interestingly, in spite of the huge industry focus on these new forms of media, in the U.S., the trend is nearly flat. In fact, there was an average decrease per six-month interval of 0.1%.

Figure 29 illustrates Internet usage by the various media generations as gathered through the SIMM data. There is a clear "digital divide" between the Internet and Computer generations and the four older generations. While one would have logically expected this, the clarity of the division is striking. We can only assume this gap in usage will only grow in the future.

This data clearly supports the concept of "digital natives" and "digital immigrants," where the Silent and Mass media generations have Internet consumption of only two-thirds or so of the Computer and Internet generations.

FIGURE 28: INTERNET USAGE TREND (IN MINUTES)

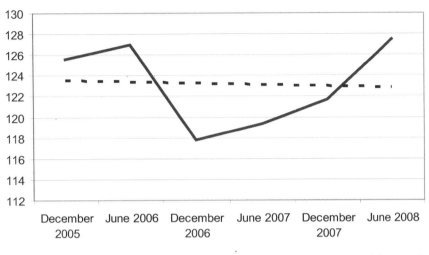

Source: BIGresearch

FIGURE 29: INTERNET USAGE BY MEDIA GENERATIONS
(JUNE 2008)

	Minutes
Silent	100.2
Mass	111.0
Space	122.7
Hippie	132.2
Computer	152.2
Internet	157.7
Total	127.5

Source: BIGresearch

Figure 30 shows the reported online entertainment activities. Shopping is the most popular activity, followed by weather, movie news, TV news and viewing photos. The research category also includes hobbies, the visit video-sharing sites include YouTube and the virtual world category includes Second Life.

FIGURE 30: ONLINE ENTERTAINMENT ACTIVITIES
(JUNE 2008)

	Percent		Percent
Shopping	40.0	Visit video-sharing sites	14.9
Weather	38.9	Stock market/business news	14.1
Movie news	28.5	Share stories with friends	13.7
TV news	28.4	Adult entertainment	13.1
View photos	25.6	Horoscopes/astrology	12.8
Sports news	24.8	Locate old friends	11.2
Video games	22.4	Fantasy sports	7.3
Research	21.1	Genealogy research	7.2
IM/chat	20.5	Gambling	7.2
Music news	20.1	Get advice from friends	6.2
Online auctions	18.1	Online dating	4.6
Celebrity gossip	17.2	Virtual world	2.3
Watch TV shows	17.1		

Source: BIGresearch

While a visual inspection of the amount of time spent, as shown above, shows a wide variation in types of uses, Figure 31 presents the results of a factor analysis that reduces the twenty-five choices to six major groups. The first factor group includes news about movies, music and television along with celebrity gossip. We have labeled this group of content Media. The second group, labeled Friends, includes sharing activities, IM and chat. The Fantasy group includes adult entertainment, fantasy sports, gambling and video games. The Facts group includes sports news, stock market and weather. Shopping speaks for itself. The last group, Nostalgia, includes horoscopes, genealogy and looking for old friends and classmates.

FIGURE 31: FACTOR ANALYSIS OF ONLINE ENTERTAINMENT ACTIVITIES (JUNE 2008)

	Media	Friends	Fantasy	Facts	Computer	Nostalgia
Movie news	0.71					
Music news	0.69					
Celebrity gossip	0.62					
TV news	0.53					
Share stories with friends		0.68				
View photos from friends		0.61				
Get advice from friends		0.57				
IM/chat		0.46				
Visit video-sharing sites		0.43				
Adult entertainment			0.56			
Fantasy sports			0.52			
Gambling			0.50			
Video games			0.48			
Online dating			0.40			
Sports news & scores				0.70		
Stock market/business news				0.64		
Weather				0.47		
Online auctions					0.70	
Shopping					0.58	
Research/get ideas for hobbies					0.57	
Horoscopes/astrology						0.56
Genealogy research						0.50
Locate old friends/classmates						0.45

Source: BIGresearch

Comparing these online entertainment activity groups to the media generations reveals how the same medium, the Internet, is used very differently. Figure 32 shows the media activity interest is high among both the Computer and Internet generations. What distinguishes the Internet Generation from the Computer Generation, though, is the former's greater interest in friend and fantasy activities. The Space Generation is near average on most activities. The Mass Generation is most interested in shopping. The Silent Generation is most interested in facts and nostalgia and has the lowest interest in fantasy.

FIGURE 32: ONLINE ENTERTAINMENT ACTIVITY FACTORS BY MEDIA GENERATIONS INDEX (JUNE 2008)

	Media	Friends	Fantasy	Facts	Shopping	Nostalgia
Silent	66	103	70	114	92	114
Mass	88	86	79	111	107	104
Space	102	85	91	106	104	100
Hippie	113	90	106	101	102	94
Computer	122	118	133	81	100	95
Internet	120	145	150	64	82	69

Source: BIGresearch

Digital Media

Digital media in the SIMM studies are defined as e-mail, instant messaging (IM), blogs and video games. This media form represents the single largest category in terms of allocated time in all the SIMM reports. As shown, there was an average total of 220.3 minutes per day devoted to digital media by SIMM respondents in June 2008. Figure 33 shows the composition of the four subcategories. What is interesting is that all four categories have maintained their relative standing compared with each other for the past four years.

FIGURE 33: DIGITAL USAGE BY TYPE (IN MINUTES)

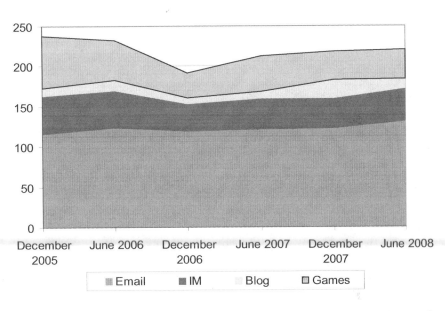

Source: BIGresearch

Figure 34 shows the total amount of time consumers spent with digital media decreasing by 1.4% over the three-year measuring period (SIMM data is in six month increments). While this is still a very small decrease, what is interesting is that it is the fastest decreasing category out of the 31 media forms studied in the SIMM file. This seems to illustrate that the category is still quite volatile. Most of the observed current decrease can be attributed to blogs and video game time.

FIGURE 34: ALL DIGITAL MEDIA USAGE TREND (IN MINUTES)

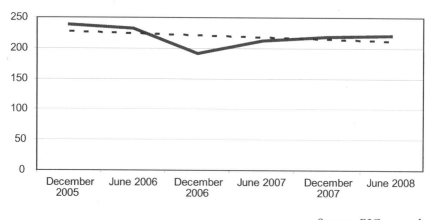

Source: BIGresearch

Figure 35 illustrates the digital media usage by the media generations. It strongly reinforces the digital divide idea that has become so popular.

The Computer and Internet generations spend nearly 300 minutes per day or more on digital media, or about five hours. This can be compared to the older generations who spend around 200 minutes per day—substantially less. The differences would be even more pronounced, if e-mail were removed from the digital media category.

FIGURE 35: DIGITAL MEDIA USAGE BY MEDIA GENERATIONS (JUNE 2008)

	E-mail	IM	Blog	Game	Digital
Silent	115.5	17.4	3.6	17.3	153.8
Mass	123.4	20.3	5.2	19.4	168.3
Space	134.1	29.8	5.9	25.5	195.3
Hippie	141.6	42.8	11.2	34.6	230.1
Computer	141.4	67.5	22.9	62.6	294.5
Internet	116.4	89.9	26.8	83.1	316.1
Total	131.3	40.7	11.7	36.6	220.3

Source: BIGresearch

Print Media

Because the three categories of print media seem to share common characteristics we have combined them for this discussion.

Newspapers, as shown in Figure 36, represent the smallest of the media consumption categories with an average daily usage of 44.8 minutes. However, what is interesting—when one considers all the poor publicity newspapers have received over the past few years—is that, according to SIMM studies, newspapers showed a 1.71% growth rate in time allocated over the past six months.

Figure 37 shows the newspaper preferences by media generations, based on the reported time spent, from the SIMM data. As can be seen, the preference for local dailies and weeklies, as indicated by the time spent with them, increases with age, with the Silent and Mass generations leading the way. It is interesting to note that the national newspapers have a different pattern, with *USA Today* and the *Wall Street Journal* showing consistent consumption patterns across all the media generations. Of particular note is the increased consumption of the *New York Times* among the Internet Generation.

FIGURE 36: NEWSPAPER USAGE TREND (IN MINUTES)

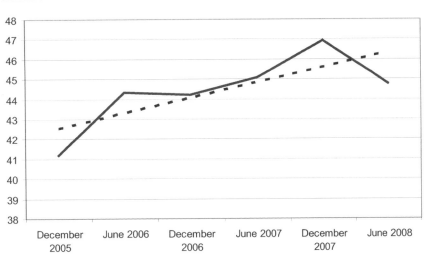

Source: BIGresearch

FIGURE 37: NEWSPAPER PREFERENCES BY MEDIA
GENERATION (JUNE 2008)

	Silent	Mass	Space	Hippie	Computer	Internet	Total
New York Times	6	6	5	6	9	11	7
USA Today	12	12	11	10	10	10	11
Wall Street Journal	7	6	6	6	7	6	6
Local dailies	52	48	44	38	30	25	40
Weekly newspapers	32	29	27	24	17	15	25

Source: BIGresearch

Magazines

The three-year period for magazine consumption, measured by the reported amount of time spent with all titles, is shown in Figure 38. Most recently, magazine usage is growing at a rate of 1.38% per six-month period. In the current SIMM period, June 2008, magazine consumption averaged 49.1 minutes per day.

FIGURE 38: MAGAZINE USAGE TREND (IN MINUTES)

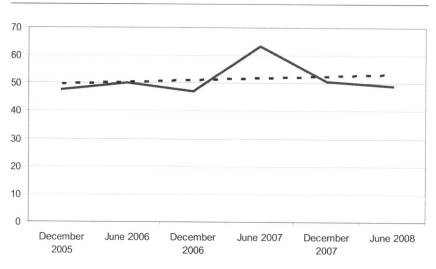

Source: BIGresearch

Figure 39 shows magazine usage, and, therefore, magazine preference by media generation. Several magazines such as *Time*, *Newsweek*, *Good Housekeeping*, and *Reader's Digest* clearly skew toward the oldest generation — the Silents. *Cosmopolitan* skews toward the Internet Generation. Thus, we can see the power of the SIMM data, if it is used by the media planners and buyers to understand not just magazine circulation, but also consumer usage of the various magazine titles.

FIGURE 39: TOP TEN MAGAZINE PREFERENCES BY MEDIA GENERATION (JUNE 2008)

	Silent	Mass	Space	Hippie	Computer	Internet	Total
People	2.3	3.2	5.6	6.5	5.9	5.3	4.9
Cosmopolitan	0.1	0.2	0.9	2.1	7.1	9.2	2.8
Time	4.1	3.0	2.3	1.7	2.0	1.9	2.4
Reader's Digest	3.7	3.4	2.7	1.9	0.6	0.4	2.2
Sports Illustrated	1.2	1.3	1.2	1.9	1.8	1.6	1.5
Good Housekeeping	3.2	2.6	1.8	1.1	0.2		1.5
Newsweek	2.4	2.0	1.2	1.2	0.9	0.6	1.4
Woman's Day	2.3	1.9	1.9	1.2	0.6	0.3	1.4
Better Homes and Gardens	0.8	1.9	2.1	1.3	0.4		1.2
Maxim	0.1	0.3	0.5	1.2	2.5	0.5	1.0

Source: BIGresearch

Direct Mail

A very important media form, not commonly measured through traditional media analysis, is direct mail. For the most part, media planners and buyers have seldom considered the amount of consumer time or attention direct mail receives from consumers. Being primarily response or results focused, that is, a sale or a movement toward a sale, direct has been hampered in the past by having a very limited view of how the medium competes in the overall media spectrum. SIMM data, however, provides an insight into direct mail that can and should be very helpful to media planners and buyers in developing integrated communication programs.

Figure 40 shows the direct mail usage amounts from the SIMM studies. The current period average for direct mail is 56.3 minutes. Most interestingly, direct mail has been the fastest growing media consumption category over the past three years as measured by SIMM data. The consumption rate of direct mail has increased by 2.76%, during the study time.

FIGURE 40: DIRECT MAIL USAGE TREND (IN MINUTES)

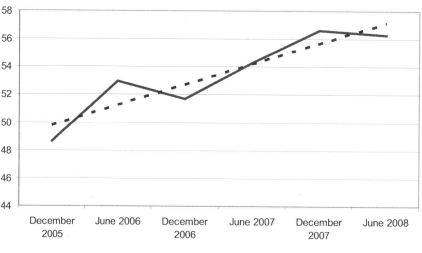

Source: BIGresearch

All three print media categories—newspapers, magazines and direct mail—show a similar pattern, that is, a drop-off in consumption among the Internet Generation. That is shown in Figure 41. Direct mail, however, increases slightly for the Mass, Space and Hippie generations.

FIGURE 41: PRINT MEDIA USAGE BY MEDIA GENERATIONS (JUNE 2008)

	Newspapers	Magazines	Direct Mail
Silent	52.3	48.5	55.3
Mass	50.5	49.4	57.6
Space	47.8	50.0	59.6
Hippie	40.3	49.8	58.2
Computer	38.6	49.0	54.1
Internet	37.7	42.8	44.6
Total	44.8	49.1	56.3

Source: BIGresearch

With this view of the consumption of specific media forms related to the concept of media generations, we now turn to an overview of all media.

Media Types

The major media categories appear to fall into two groups, based upon the historical changes over the past three years. The Internet, digital media, magazines and TV all seem to share the same characteristics of relatively low half-year-to-half-year growth and very low correlation coefficients (R^2) with the number of months measured. A high correlation would mean a linear trend in one direction or the other, i.e., up or down. Low correlation signifies volatility, or measurable up and down movement, in the usage levels from one study to another. It is this volatility which should be of interest to media planners and buyers. The media marketplace is certainly not static and assuming that media values are consistent could create major errors in media planning and buying.

Figure 42 shows the summaries for the seven categories. As shown, those categories—Internet, digital, magazines and TV—all share low growth and high volatility. That would seem to mean that consumers are selecting those media forms because of current content or perceived content over time. For example, given the importance of newsstand sales of magazines, it is reasonable to assume the magazine is selected because of the content in that issue, for example, a "swimsuit edition" or other attractive content feature. We hypothesize that other media in this category are likely selected for the same reason, such as a favorite TV show or a well-known Web site. Thus, we have characterized these media forms as being primarily content oriented.

The other three categories — newspapers, radio and direct mail — all rely on a dependable stream of material. Radio is tuned to a particular frequency or station with the expectation that the media experience will have some benefit to the consumer. Similarly, a newspaper is chosen for its overall value rather than a particular news story. The mailbox fills with catalogs for those consumers who are mail shoppers. Here, we argue, the choice is based on the media channel, rather than on the specific content of the media form that is most critical. If our hypothesis is correct, it does much to explain why these media forms are less volatile because that is in their very nature.

FIGURE 42: MEDIA USAGE TYPES (JUNE 2008)

	Min	Max	Current	Percent	R^2
Content Media					
Internet	117.8	127.5	127.5	-.11	.004
Digital	191.7	238.0	220.3	-1.40	.125
Magazines	47.1	63.4	49.1	1.38	.048
TV	126.7	137.1	129.6	.63	.144
Channel Media					
Newspaper	41.2	46.9	44.8	1.71	.581
Radio	85.2	129.9	129.9	1.42	.797
Direct	48.7	56.6	56.3	2.76	.847

Source: BIGresearch

This type of analysis can be very helpful to media planners for it provides a new and different view of how media are used and, thus, how the marketer might improve the media plans going forward.

Simultaneous Usage

A major area of interest, which was alluded to earlier in this chapter, is simultaneous media usage. That simply means consumers are multi-tasking during their media consumption activities. For example, they may be online, listening to or monitoring the television, flipping through a magazine *and* talking on a cell phone all at the same time, a not-unheard-of feat for most of today's teenagers.

If all the media categories, reported in the consumption and usage section of the SIMM report are aggregated, the average total media consumption by person is 757.5 minutes, or 12.6 hours, per day. This clearly illustrates that for this type of media consumption to be possible, some of the media usage must be accomplished while the respondent is engaged in other media activities.

While this simultaneous media usage is commonly recognized in advertising and marketing circles, it is totally ignored in the current media measures; television viewing is still estimated separately and independently, as is radio, and as are newspapers and magazines. In short, the industry is plagued with historical measurement approaches that have little or no relevance to the way people actually consume media in today's marketplace. Radio, for example, has long been characterized as a secondary medium. Listeners commonly engage in other activities while still enjoying the programming. Every media planner and buyer knows this. Yet, radio is still measured on the basis of intra-media comparisons — what station is being listened to — rather than a more relevant inter-media basis, namely, its usage in combination with other media forms.

Monochronic vs. Polychronic Media Consumer Behavior

Two concepts not often referenced in media planning are monochronic and polychronic information processing by media users. Quite simply, these terms describe how people use their time and how they process information. People who are monochronic processors tend to use their time sequentially, that is, they do one thing, then another, in some sort of sequence. Polychronic processors, however, deal with information and activities in parallel. Simply put, they multitask with media forms—listening to the radio while going through the direct mail and scanning e-mail, all simultaneously. The Silent and Mass generations were taught initially to read, a sequential activity, one word following another, one page after another and one chapter after another. So, they tend to be monochronic information processors. Digital natives—those who grew up with television, computers, cell phones and the like—are generally polychronic processors. The relevance of these two concepts becomes quite clear when we start to look at simultaneous media consumption.

Media planners, and certainly those who measure media distribution, seemingly have assumed that all mass media are consumed one at a time, that is, monochronically. That is clearly apparent in the way they identify and measure audience media involvement and activity. The inherent bias in the audience measurement systems is that people exposed to television programming—and, therefore, television commercials—can or will do nothing else at that time. It is assumed that they are totally engaged with that single medium. Anyone who has ever watched television knows this is not right, yet, when it comes to media planning, we toss out all we know about how people behave and slavishly follow the measurement systems devised fifty or more years ago. At that time, single focused attention by individuals and perhaps even families may have occurred in some households but those days are long gone.

The idea that a medium can be consumed polychronically, that is, in combination with other media forms is new in the media lexicon. Watching television, for example, is commonly accompanied with on-line activity at the same time. That is clearly shown in the SIMM data that follows. This idea of simultaneous consumption of media—consuming more than one medium at the same time, polychronically—is still a relatively new area for traditional media planning. We first reported and demonstrated this phenomenon in a paper presented at the ARF in 2002 and at the ARF Think Conference in 2003. It has since been demonstrated in SIMM studies and reported at three ESOMAR media planning and allocation conferences in Geneva, 2004, Montreal, 2005 and Shanghai, 2006. Thus, while simultaneous media consumption by consumers is not a new idea and is widely recognized in the literature and in trade publications, it has been slow to develop in media planning and buying circles. Unfortunately, media planners have seemingly preferred to maintain the individual intra-media measures to which they are accustomed.

In the SIMM studies, the most common media usage combination is going online, then turning on the TV and paying attention to both at the same time. Figure 43, which shows the most current SIMM studied figures, shows this polychronic behavior: 38% of respondents have gone online first and then engaged in television viewing. This is the sort of information that is missing from most media planning and buying approaches today. One of the key points of this simultaneous usage is that the SIMM data shows that when questioned about media behavior in the "other direction"—that is watching TV and *then* going online—only 26% of respondents report this behavior (also in Figure 43).

This is a key finding from the SIMM studies. People clearly have a primary medium, which they are using, and a secondary medium to which they are also attending, for example, "I'm online, but I'm also monitoring television," or "I'm watching TV, but I'm also monitoring the Web and my e-mail." Thus, consumers have created what we have termed "foreground" and "background" media for themselves. Importantly, only they know which is which during what period of time. This is an area that has been totally neglected in media planning and buying. SIMM studies are the only research technique that enables the marketer to know and understand what is truly happening in the media marketplace.

When you are online are you also watching TV? This generally appears in most charts when we are reporting Simultaneous Media Usage.

FIGURE 43: U.S. MEDIA FORMS USED TOGETHER (JUNE 2008)
Primary Medium (Regularly only)

	Online	TV	Mags	News	Direct	Cell	Radio
Online		26	6	8	10	14	17
TV	38		20	24	21	15	8
Mags	7	10				5	8
News	10	12				5	11
Direct	21	14				7	11
Radio	22	4	12	13	12	12	

Source: BIGresearch

Averaging the simultaneous media usage behavior across all media to facilitate relevant comparisons yields an overall average of 16.3% (as shown in Figure 44). Comparing this across media generations shows the Computer Generation with the highest rate of simultaneous consumption. The Internet Generation shows a small decrease probably because they watch less television. Of special note, is the much lower figure for the Silent Generation. Clearly, they have maintained their monochronic processing methods in which they were initially trained as children. From this, it is easy to see why traditional media measurement systems were developed in the mid-twentieth century. They made sense then, but they are totally obsolete now.

FIGURE 44: AVERAGE SIMULTANEOUS CONSUMPTION PERCENTAGE BY MEDIA GENERATION

	Percent Simultaneous
Silent	12.7
Mass	15.2
Space	16.4
Hippie	16.4
Computer	18.5
Internet	17.2
Total	16.3

Source: BIGresearch

With this view of how consumers actually use media, not how syndicated services estimate their usage, we move to a totally new measure that becomes possible from SIMM data—media influence.

References

Schultz, Don E. and Joseph J. Pilotta "Developing the Foundation for a New Approach to Understanding How Media Advertising Works," 3rd Annual ESOMAR/ARF World Audience Measurement Conference, June 13-18, 2004, Geneva.

Pilotta, J. J., Schultz, D. E., Drenik, G. & Rist, P. (2004). "Simultaneous media usage: A critical consumer orientation to media planning." *Journal of Consumer Behavior,* Volume 3, Issue 3, 285-292.

Schultz, Don E., Joseph J. Pilotta and Martin P. Block, "Implementing a Media Consumption Model," 4th Annual ESOMAR/ARF World Audience Measurement Conference, June 22-24, 2005, Montreal.

Schultz, Don E., Joseph J. Pilotta and Martin P. Block, "Media Consumption and Purchasing," ESOMAR M3 Conference, June, 2006, Shanghai.

Chapter

6

Media Influence

About a half dozen years ago, media engagement became a hot topic in media circles. Recognizing that the growing multitude of media forms couldn't be evaluated using traditional systems, media measurement organizations and media researchers proposed the concept of "media engagement." In simple terms, an attempt is made to determine what media forms are most attractive to consumers and, to which they give the most attention. Hopefully, by knowing the level of consumer engagement, the media planner can assume the media form itself adds value to the advertising message. Thus, media engagement has become a major topic in media planning circles. Attempts have been made to use engagement as a key criterion variable in solving the problem of inter-media comparison in spite of the fact that methods of measuring engagement are still being developed.

This idea of engagement—or, more practically, media attention—is the one single measure that appears to be consistent across all media categories. As Figure 45 shows, most consumers pay little attention to advertising. With 5% or less of the viewing audience paying full attention to what is occurring on the television screen, understanding media engagement becomes a major media decision point. Put another way, the media form becomes important when the consumer deems it important and considers it to be influential on their purchase decisions, not when the marketer invests the greatest amount of the advertising budget in it.

FIGURE 45: PAYING ATTENTION TO TV COMMERCIALS? (JUNE 2008)

Don't regularly or occasionally	Percent
Fully attend commercial	95.5
Leave the room	93.8
Talk with others	92.5
Mentally tune out	88.4
Read magazine or book	75.0
Go online	65.7

Source: BIGresearch

A more important measure is one developed by BIGresearch and measured through the SIMM data: how influential is the media form in helping you make decisions about what products or services to purchase. We argue this is a much more important view of the media than simply which ones the consumer likes or which ones they prefer. The primary importance in measuring media audiences to marketers is whether or not the product or service is seen or attended to, not whether or not the media form was enjoyed. Thus, for the past three years, SIMM data has included questions on the importance the media has on helping consumers make decisions about product purchasing.

Figure 46 shows the average percent of historical influences across twenty media and marketing communication categories. While there is some up and down movement, the patterns in the data have been relatively stable over the past three years. There are some differences, however, that merit further discussion.

FIGURE 46: AVERAGE MEDIA INFLUENCES (PERCENTAGES)

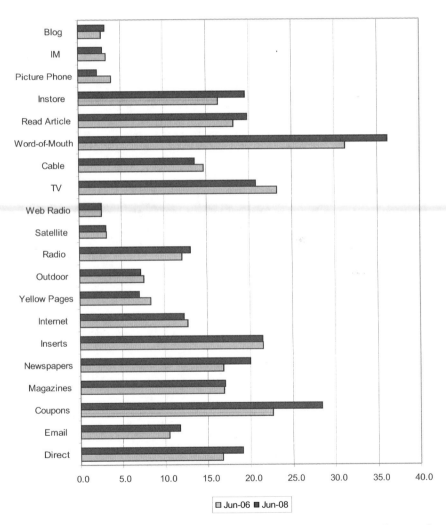

Source: BIGresearch

Figure 47 shows the percentage of consumers that report the impact of various media communication activities on their purchase decisions. As shown, word of mouth is the media form consumers report has the greatest influence on their purchasing decisions with just over 36% of the sample selecting it. The next two categories are "below-the-line" activities—coupons and inserts. While media planners may have some indirect influence on these forms of media, they are not considered "media" in many planning approaches. Thus, we begin to see the importance of viewing media and communication in a very broad way, not just the traditional forms of television, radio and magazines and even with the addition of the new digital media forms of Internet, mobile and the like. Perhaps a better term than media would be "brand contact points" as some writers have suggested.

Near the bottom of the media forms that influence consumer's purchase decisions are categories such as texting and advertisements in video games at around 2%. These are low not because their impact is unimportant but because they currently have very low utilization. As usage of these new forms of media grow, their importance will likely grow as well. Note: The base in the media influence chart below is always the total sample from the SIMM studies, much like a television rating.

Comparing the month-to-month growth rates over the past three years of SIMM data shows a somewhat different picture, however. Figure 48 shows blogs, coupons and in-store promotion growing in influence. Television is declining the most rapidly, at 4.7% every six months. So, while television audiences may be stable or ever growing, the impact of television in the key area of influence on purchase decisions seems to be declining rather dramatically.

FIGURE 47: AVERAGE INFLUENCE BY MARKETING COMMUNICATION ACTIVITY (JUNE 2008)

	Percent
Word of mouth	36.23
Coupons	28.38
Inserts	21.51
TV	20.82
Newspapers	19.97
Read an article	19.79
In-store	19.56
Direct mail	19.09
Magazines	17.03
Cable	13.64
Radio	13.07
Internet	12.27
E-mail	11.7
Product placement	9.01
Outdoor	7.22
Yellow Pages	7.01
Blogs	3.14
Satellite	3.12
IM	2.86
Web radio	2.65
Text	2.49
Games	2.38
Picture phone	2.2

Source: BIGresearch

FIGURE 48: AVERAGE 3-YEAR INFLUENCE GROWTH RATE BY MARKETING COMMUNICATION ACTIVITY (JUNE 2008)

	Percent	Growth Rate
Growing		
Blogs	3.1	5.85
Coupons	28.4	4.89
In-store	19.6	4.02
Direct mail	19.1	3.32
Newspapers	20.0	3.17
Web radio	2.7	3.02
Word of mouth	36.2	2.58
E-mail	11.7	2.57
Satellite	3.1	2.37
Radio	13.1	1.85
Read article	19.8	1.83
Steady		
IM	2.9	0.80
Inserts	21.5	0.45
Magazines	17.0	0.03
Outdoor	7.2	-0.70
Declining		
Internet	12.3	-1.60
Cable	13.6	-2.57
Yellow Pages	7.0	-2.61
Picture phone	2.2	-2.63
TV	20.8	-3.73

Source: BIGresearch

It is also important to consider the relative pattern of change as shown in Figure 49. Coupons and TV are stable, also meaning that the

TV decline has been consistent over the past three years. The Internet, inserts and magazines have been up and down in the past three years showing rapid changes from one study period to another.

FIGURE 49: AVERAGE 3-YEAR INFLUENCE VOLATILITY BY MARKETING COMMUNICATION ACTIVITY (JUNE 2008)

	Percent	R^2
Stable		
Coupons	28.4	0.80
TV	20.8	0.77
Word of mouth	36.2	0.75
Direct mail	19.1	0.73
Newspapers	20.0	0.72
E-mail	11.7	0.71
In-store	19.6	0.70
Moderate		
Radio	13.1	0.61
Read an article	19.8	0.58
Blogs	3.1	0.55
Cable	13.6	0.53
Yellow Pages	7.0	0.50
Volatile		
Web radio	2.7	0.22
Satellite	3.1	0.19
Internet	12.3	0.17
Outdoor	7.2	0.11
Picture phone	2.2	0.03
IM	2.9	0.02
Inserts	21.5	0.02
Magazines	17.0	0.00

Source: BIGresearch

FIGURE 50: MEDIA CATEGORY INFLUENCE BY MEDIA GENERATION (JUNE 2008)

	Silent	Mass	Space	Hippie	Computer	Internet	Total
Word of mouth	28.8	36.1	37.7	37.6	37.9	34.4	36.2
Coupons	21.1	27.7	29.8	30.9	29.8	26.0	28.4
Inserts	21.2	25.3	24.5	21.3	17.4	14.3	21.5
TV	14.7	20.3	22.6	21.9	22.1	21.7	20.9
Newspaper	25.2	24.1	21.4	17.8	15.5	14.2	20.0
Read an article	19.4	22.4	21.3	19.0	17.7	15.8	19.8
In-store	15.5	19.4	21.1	20.4	20.4	17.0	19.6
Direct mail	17.3	19.8	20.7	20.0	18.3	15.7	19.1
Magazines	13.2	16.2	16.8	17.9	18.8	18.4	17.1
Cable	7.5	11.1	13.4	14.4	17.6	18.6	13.7
Radio	8.2	11.4	13.7	14.1	15.2	15.3	13.1
Internet	7.7	10.6	11.0	12.1	16.1	17.7	12.3
E-mail	8.1	11.0	12.1	12.7	12.9	12.3	11.7
Placement	5.7	7.8	8.7	8.7	11.7	12.4	9.1
Outdoor	3.5	5.1	6.6	7.5	10.2	12.3	7.3
Yellow Pages	7.1	7.0	6.7	6.2	7.6	8.7	7.1
Blogs	1.0	1.7	2.0	3.2	5.6	6.9	3.2
Satellite	1.5	2.2	2.4	3.6	4.6	5.3	3.1
IM	1.3	1.5	2.0	2.7	4.8	7.1	2.9
Web radio	0.9	1.5	1.5	2.8	4.7	6.1	2.7
Text	0.7	1.2	1.4	2.4	4.6	6.8	2.5
Games	0.7	1.1	1.3	2.5	4.3	6.1	2.4
Video	0.7	1.3	1.3	2.1	3.8	5.4	2.2

Source: BIGresearch

One of the greatest advantages of the SIMM data is that it allows us to convert the data above for the entire population to the various media generations that have been identified. Figure 50 shows the relative influence by media generations. Figure 51 shows the categories that are relatively high among each of the generations. Not only do the categories change, but also the number of categories. The Computer and Internet generations appear to be much easier to influence through the media forms they use and claim connections to a much wider variety of media, especially the digital ones, than do some of the other groups. As shown, only the Silent Generation say they are influenced more than average by the newspaper.

FIGURE 51: HIGH INFLUENCE CATEGORIES BY MEDIA GENERATIONS

Silent	Mass	Space	Hippie	Computer	Internet
Newspaper	Newspaper	Inserts	Satellite	Text	Text
	Inserts	TV	Coupons	Games	Games
		Read	Radio	Blogs	IM
		In-store	Web	Radio	Video
		Direct	Video	Web	Radio
			Newspaper	IM	Blogs
				Satellite	Outdoor
				Outdoor	Satellite
				Internet	Internet
				Placement	Placement
				Cable	Cable
				Radio	Yellow
				Magazines	Radio
				E-mail	Magazines
				Yellow	

What is most interesting about the table above is the wide variety of media that influence the Computer and Internet generations and the low number of media for the Silent and Mass groups. Clearly, media is becoming more important to younger consumers, but their attention is divided across a broad array of media forms. This provides more evidence of the need for inter-media comparisons rather than the intra-media comparisons, which have been the common rule.

Figure 52 shows the differences by media generation based on a comparison of the influence of content- versus channel-oriented media and other approaches. Content media are the average of Internet, e-mail, IM, blogs, games, magazines, TV and cable. Channel media are the average of newspaper, radio, Web radio, satellite radio and direct mail. Promotion is the average of coupons and inserts. The ratio compares the relative influence of the two types of media. This adjusts for the lower proneness to influence that occurs among the older generations.

FIGURE 52: Media Type Influence Comparison by Media Generation (June 2008)

	Silent	Mass	Space	Hippie	Computer	Internet	Total
Content media	6.8	9.2	10.1	10.9	12.8	13.6	10.5
Channel media	10.6	11.8	11.9	11.6	11.6	11.3	11.6
Ratio (content/channel)	0.64	0.78	0.85	0.94	1.10	1.20	0.91
Word of mouth	28.8	36.1	37.7	37.6	37.9	34.4	36.2
Promotion	21.1	26.5	27.2	26.1	23.6	20.2	24.9
In-store	15.5	19.4	21.1	20.4	20.4	17.0	19.6
Text	0.7	1.2	1.4	2.4	4.6	6.8	2.5

Source: BIGresearch

It is clear that content-oriented media increase in importance among the younger generations. Older generations are more focused on channel media.

Content media and channel media provide another alternative method for media planners and buyers to consider media outlet in making decisions. It is this ability to develop multiple analytical methods that illustrates the value of SIMM data analysis, rather than sheer audience numbers or intra-media comparisons among television stations or magazine titles. SIMM data analysis moves the entire area of media planning, buying and measurement up to the strategic level in the organization rather than being simply an analytical exercise using standardized syndicated media studies.

Of growing importance in today's retail-driven marketplace, where major chains control huge shares of overall consumer spending, is the impact and effect of in-store promotional activities. Figure 53 shows the relative influence of various retail promotions by media generation. The chart should be interpreted as providing a view of the percent of each media generation saying which retail activity influences them the most in terms of their purchasing decision.

As shown below, the younger media generations appear to be much more responsive to in-store promotions than are the older ones, especially the Silent and Mass generations. Whether this is the result of the younger media generations being much more active in the marketplace or whether there are other, more fundamental, reasons is not known. Suffice it to say, that the development of in-store promotions is a much more complicated task today than simply saying, "Let's do an end-aisle," or "Let's lay down some floor graphics." The SIMM data does, however, start to provide greater insight into the impact and effect of in-store promotions than simply measuring the number who pass by the shelf-sticker or RFID tag in the store.

FIGURE 53: RETAIL THEATER INFLUENCE BY MEDIA
GENERATION (JUNE 2008)

	Silent	Mass	Space	Hippie	Computer	Internet	Total
Samples to home	15.7	25.3	31.4	31.6	30.4	23.2	27.6
Samples in store	17.0	23.7	28.2	28.0	30.0	31.2	26.5
Reading labels	23.1	24.8	24.3	20.7	20.3	18.1	22.4
Loyalty cards	15.2	20.5	21.4	21.7	21.2	14.4	20.2
Shelf coupons	12.2	16.9	20.7	20.5	21.1	13.2	18.6
Samples online	8.3	15.6	18.6	19.9	21.4	16.2	17.6
In-store flyers	12.7	16.7	19.0	18.0	17.4	13.4	16.9
Special displays	7.8	13.0	16.1	16.8	18.4	16.6	15.2
Coupons at register	8.5	10.0	11.5	13.1	14.0	9.0	11.6
In-store events	5.4	9.6	11.1	12.6	14.1	15.4	11.4
Ads on shelves	4.6	8.0	11.1	11.5	11.9	8.2	9.8
In-store signage	4.1	8.0	9.9	10.4	12.1	9.0	9.4
Parking lot events	2.3	5.4	6.7	7.6	10.2	8.7	7.0
In-store television	1.2	2.8	3.8	5.0	8.2	10.3	4.9
In-store radio	1.1	2.8	3.7	4.9	7.2	8.4	4.5
Check-out ads	0.9	2.5	2.8	4.6	6.0	5.1	3.7
Information kiosks	1.1	2.5	3.0	3.5	5.1	5.5	3.4
Floor graphics	1.4	2.2	3.1	3.3	4.6	5.0	3.2
Shopping cart ads	0.5	1.8	2.3	3.1	4.4	4.6	2.8

Source: BIGresearch

Summary

This chapter has provided the basic elements of how the SIMM data can be used to provide more sophisticated approaches to media planning and buying. It demonstrates that media planners need more today than the simple intra-media analysis on which the industry has been built. Given the wide range of media alternatives, for example, thirty-one in the current SIMM database, it is clear that inter-media measures are much more critical. Further, the development of the media generations concept provides a unique approach to rethinking the entire media planning and buying methodology. In the next chapter, we take the next step in revising media planning and buying—how media might be allocated based on their influence on consumers.

Chapter

7

Allocating Media by Influence

Based on the preceding chapters, using the media generations concept and the media influence on purchase by category data, as gathered by BIGresearch through the SIMM studies, the next question is how these new techniques can be used to improve media planning, allocation and measurement. In this chapter, we illustrate the value of the Media Generations approach through an application to the automobile category.

Applying the New Media Planning Concepts

On June 23, 2008, *Advertising Age* reported the estimated media spending for the top 100 national advertisers for 2007. The total, as shown in Figure 54, was estimated to be $61 billion. Television was the dominant advertising medium with nearly 57% of the total, followed by magazines and newspapers. Internet spending was estimated to be slightly over $4 billion, or nearly 7% of the total.

FIGURE 54: 2007 TOP 100 ADVERTISER MEDIA SPENDING

	Millions of Dollars	Percent
Magazines	10,801	17.6
Newspaper	7,209	11.8
Outdoor	1,038	1.7
TV	34,826	56.8
Radio	3,226	5.3
Internet	4,184	6.8
All Measured Media	61,283	100.0

Advertising Age — TNS

Among the top 100 advertisers are seven car and truck manufacturers. The car and truck spending totals are shown in Figure 55. As can be seen, over $8 billion was spent in this category. While car and truck manufacturers tend to spend relatively more in television, at approximately 64% of their total advertising investment, the category fairly closely resembles the average expenditure by all advertisers—they spend a near average proportion on the Internet, $558 million or about 7% of their total, for example. Thus, we believe it can be used as a relevant example.

FIGURE 55: 2007 AUTO ADVERTISERS (TOP SEVEN) AMONG TOP 100 MEDIA SPENDING

	Millions of Dollars	Percent
Magazines	1,507	18.4
Newspaper	538	6.6
Outdoor	119	1.5
TV	5,206	63.6
Radio	252	3.1
Internet	558	6.8
All Measured Media	8,180	100.0

Advertising Age — TNS

As shown, when comparing Figures 54 and 55, the car and truck category mirrors the overall media investment for all advertisers in terms of the media they selected and the investments they made.

Figure 56 shows the seven car and truck advertisers described in Figure 55. We should note that each manufacturer spend includes multiple nameplates — Honda, for example, includes both Honda and Acura.

In the chart, individual spending by manufacturer has been converted to a percentage of the total spend of the top seven auto manufacturers to obtain a share of voice (SOV) estimate. For example, among the top seven, Ford accounts for 20.3% of the dollars spent.

Note: The SOV shown here is not the share of the total spend for the car and truck category, but only the SOV among the top seven advertisers, which is more relevant for comparison.

Adding In Purchase Intentions

In the chart, the first choice is the name of the car that consumers say they are considering purchasing or leasing within the next six months. This data is drawn from the BIGresearch SIMM study for the past six months. Again, all product brand names are aggregated to the manufacturer and then the percentage has been calculated. As shown, General Motors has a 24% SOV and a 26% first choice proportion. From that, we have calculated a simple ratio, in this case, 1.08. That shows that the choice preference percentage is slightly higher than the SOV spend. In other words, GM is generating more preference with their advertising dollars than one would expect simply because preference is greater than spend.

As shown below, Honda appears to be the most efficient car and truck advertiser with a ratio of 1.40, with Toyota next at 1.27. Certainly, other factors are in play here — promotions, discounts, dealer programs and the like. It is clear, however, that marketing communication efforts across the car and truck manufacturers vary and vary widely. Thus, some manufacturers are getting "more bang for the buck," to use a trite phrase, for their advertising spend.

FIGURE 56: 2007 Auto Share of Voice* and Reported First Choice in Next 6 months**

	SOV	1st Choice	Ratio
General Motors Corp.	24.2	26.2	1.08
Ford Motor Co.	20.3	17.9	0.88
Toyota Motor Corp.	14.1	18.0	1.27
Chrysler	14.0	13.3	0.95
Nissan Motor Co.	11.4	7.0	0.62
Honda Motor Co.	10.7	14.9	1.40
Hyundai Motor Co.	5.2	2.6	0.49

Source: BIGresearch

Bringing media spend into the consideration requires some additional assumptions. Figure 57 shows cost per thousand (CPM) estimates for the various media across auto manufacturer categories. The costs are averages across demographic categories in the case of magazines and dayparts in the case of television. The Internet CPM is an average of banners, video pre-rolls and other video content. Certainly, these can be easily changed to suit the need, requirements or even the experience of any marketer. The costs also reflect the broadest (all adult) target audiences, and are intended only for comparative purposes and not developing a specific media plan.

---

*   2007 TNS based on the seven manufacturers

** Includes all brands for each manufacturer and excludes other manufacturers' brands, SIMM, June 2008

Including the SIMM Data Media Influence

The influence proportions shown in Figure 57 are averaged across the eight product categories discussed in the previous chapter. The highest influence is newspaper inserts followed by television. Adjusting the influence by the cost to get cost-per-thousand dollars influence, we find magazines provide the most influence per dollar invested, for example, the CPM of $12.68 in magazines yields 17.05 influence points among the 1,000 individuals, or 13.45 influence points per dollar. Television on the other hand, yields only 7.78 influence points per dollar. Product placement is by far the least efficient with only 1.3 influence points per dollar.

FIGURE 57: COST WEIGHTED BY INFLUENCE

	CPM	Influence	Influence Points/$1000
Magazines	12.68	17.05	13.45
Inserts	16.00	21.49	13.43
Outdoor	7.35	7.26	9.88
Radio	14.43	13.08	9.06
Internet	15.33	12.33	8.04
TV	26.84	20.89	7.78
Newspapers	33.18	19.98	6.02
Email	20.00	11.73	5.87
Blogs	9.00	3.17	3.52
Satellite	9.00	3.13	3.48
Product placement	70.00	9.10	1.30

Source: BIGresearch

To illustrate how these types of calculations can work, we have taken additional information from the most recent SIMM study. Shown in Figure 58 are people who have said they plan to purchase or lease a car or truck in the next six months. Figure 58 shows that 11.4% are planning such a purchase or lease.

FIGURE 58: PLANNING TO PURCHASE/LEASE A CAR OR TRUCK IN THE NEXT 6 MONTHS (JUNE 2008)

	Percent
Plan to purchase (planners)	11.4
Don't plan to purchase	88.6

Source: BIGresearch

By changing the media influence to the car and truck category only, as shown in Figure 60, we can then estimate the optimal allocation of the media spend against this target of "prospective buyer in the next six months." This is done on the basis of media influence.

The process, since it is so different from present-day media allocation approaches, probably deserves a repeat discussion. The first step is to select a target market. In this case, it is those planning to lease or purchase a car or truck in the next six months. For all practical purposes, this could be any target market the advertiser might determine. It could be category purchasers, brand purchasers or even a demographic category.

The second step is determining the influence, either average or category specific, for the selected target market. Also, in this step, it is necessary to determine the media category usage and the relative costs. In this case, the usage (in minutes per day) is for the planned car and truck purchasers as shown in Figure 59. The costs are generally based on all adult CPMs. Other costs could be used depending on the nature of the media buy.

Step three is to estimate the influence per dollar for each media category and weight the categories by the relative usage. This provides a weighted influence-per-dollar that can then be converted into a percentage to show the optimal allocation across the various media categories. Figure 61 shows the results of these types of optimizing calculations for the planned purchasers in the car and truck category in the next six months.

FIGURE 59: PARAMETERS FOR PLANNERS

	All auto influence	Planner influence	Usage	CPM
TV	21.4	31.0	139.0	26.84
Newspapers	19.6	29.2	54.1	33.18
Magazines	16.1	25.8	58.4	12.68
Radio	14.2	22.9	102.0	14.43
Internet	10.7	18.5	147.3	15.33
Outdoor	10.3	17.2	14.4	7.35

Source: BIGresearch

FIGURE 60: OPTIMAL DOLLAR ALLOCATION FOR CAR AND TRUCK PURCHASE PLANNERS (JUNE 2008)

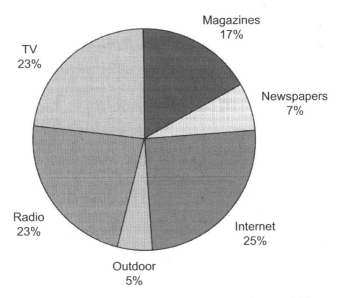

Source: BIGresearch

The results of the media influence-driven allocation approach, derived from the SIMM data, are quite different from those traditionally used by car and truck manufacturers. That difference can be seen by comparing Figure 61 with the Figure 55. Figure 55 illustrates the traditional pattern of media allocation by these marketers.

Some assumptions are made to develop this illustration and they should be pointed out. First, we assume the car and truck manufacturers are targeting those consumers that are planning a car or truck purchase in the next six months—in other words, they are seeking short-term returns. The actual targets of the manufacturers may be different. Thus, the overall advertising and promotion strategy of the company would have to be taken into account.

It is also assumed all minutes with media are of equal value, that is, the attention paid to radio by minute would be the same value as a minute for a magazine or for television. Certainly an adjustment could be made, if it is believed this equality of minutes is not correct.

Figure 61 compares the historical allocation of advertising by auto manufacturers with the estimated optimal allocation developed from the media influence data from the SIMM studies. From that, it would appear car and truck manufacturers are overspending in television and under spending in both radio and the Internet.

FIGURE 61: COMPARISON OF CAR AND TRUCK MANUFACTURER ADVERTISING[*] AND THE OPTIMAL ALLOCATION

	2007[**]$	Pct	Optimal$	Pct	Change$
Internet	558	6.8	2,079	25.4	1,521
Radio	252	3.1	1,891	23.1	1,639
TV	5,206	63.6	1,874	22.9	-3,332
Magazines	1,507	18.4	1,386	16.9	-121
Newspaper	538	6.6	556	6.8	18
Outdoor	119	1.5	393	4.8	274

Source: BIGresearch

[*]   Top 7 auto advertisers from top 100 list
[**] Millions

The real value of the new media influence data for media planners and buyers is not just that certain media are over-invested or under-invested, but, as the last column shows, one can see by how much. Thus, the planner or buyer, using this type of allocation approach, would have an idea of the amount of money in play. Given the differences shown for newspaper and outdoor, few changes would need to be made. The same might be true for magazines. The real opportunity appears to be a better allocation and alignment between Internet, radio and TV spend and the potential return.

The problem, of course, is that while the SIMM data is gathered every six months, media plans are generally based on longer periods of time. Thus, a rolling evaluation of consumer purchase intentions and media influence would provide a window into the future in which media planners could have an ongoing model of changes that need to be made in almost real time. This would seem to be far better than the annual approaches presently in use.

Adding In Media Generations

Taking this media analysis a step further, the optimal media allocations also change by media generations. Figure 62 shows the distribution of the media generations. The proportions shown here include a truncation of the Internet Generation to include only those 18 and older, as they are the most likely purchasers of a car or truck.

FIGURE 62: MEDIA GENERATIONS (JUNE 2008)

	Percent
Silent	19.2
Mass	18.8
Space	15.5
Hippie	18.4
Computer	24.4
Internet	3.7

Source: BIGresearch

When we take the media generation figures and optimize the media spend based on those, we arrive at the optimal allocation as shown in Figure 63. As shown, television, magazines and newspapers all decline in value to the marketer as the generations become younger. Internet increases, with the proportion double among the youngest generation (Internet) compared with the oldest generation (Silent). Radio increases slightly among the middle generations (Space and Hippie).

FIGURE 63: OPTIMAL ALLOCATION PERCENTAGE BY MEDIA GENERATIONS AVERAGE INFLUENCE (JUNE 2008)

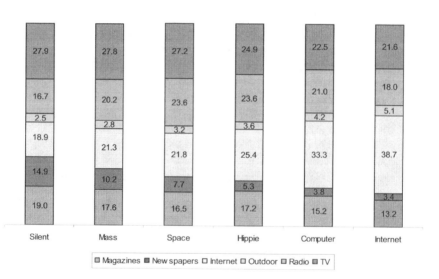

Source: BIGresearch

The information contained in the chart above should be very useful to media planners and buyers. It in essence is a media allocation roadmap—something not available until now. As shown, the various media forms are optimized, as is the allocation among media generations. The insight provided is even more important when considered against various target markets. While demographics have been used for years, the ability to connect media influence with the new and important media generation concept enhances the media planning and buying algorithm substantially.

Figure 64 shows all of the elements that could be incorporated into an expanded and fully functioning marketing communication spending allocation model.

FIGURE 64: MARKETING COMMUNICATION ALLOCATION MODEL

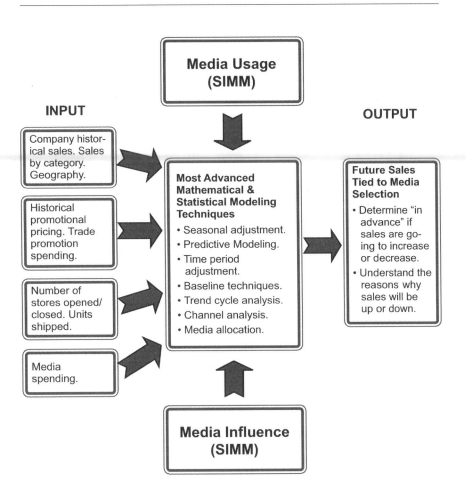

The model above takes media planning and allocation to the next level. It incorporates all the traditional inputs media planners and buyers have used in the past—historical sales, promotional pricing, stores/units/dealers or other distribution forms and previous media investments.

These are then combined with the SIMM media usage information, which includes combinations of media and simultaneous media usage.

Coming from the other side is the SIMM data, which provides information on the influence of the media form on purchase decisions by media category.

All that information is then combined through various mathematical approaches, either in use or available to the planner or modeler, such as baselining, trend cycle analysis and predictive modeling, to make the best use of the data.

The output, as shown, provides a future sales projection, tied to media allocation; something media planners, buyers and their marketing partners have long dreamed of, but, until now, has not been possible. The new consumer-centric media allocation approach answers many of the questions that have always been asked. The only decision now is how and where to implement the methodology.

Chapter

8

Summary

The greatest challenge for media planners and buyers has always been "which" and "what" media forms were most used by consumers. When this is known, the allocation of media funds becomes a much easier task and a more effective use of marketer and advertiser dollars.

In the beginning, media allocation was a rather simple matter. Limited media forms and the thirst for knowledge and information by consumers almost guaranteed media exposure and, therefore, advertising exposure. As media forms increased, advertisers and their agencies began to rely more and more on surrogate measures such as print distribution and estimated readers and pass-along audiences, set-on measures for broadcast and cars passing intersections for outdoor. Good estimates, but not terribly relevant or helpful to the media planner.

Recently, the advertising industry has focused more and more on technology to identify audiences. People meters, set-top boxes, eye cameras, RFID and on and on, all have been tested, but with limited success. More recently, the concept of a "day in the life of" measures have emerged, where researchers trail consumers through the day, noting their use of media in a supposedly unobtrusive way.

In spite of all these efforts, marketers, their agencies and even the media themselves know little about actual consumer use or consumption of media beyond the traditional syndicated measures. The reason: only the consumer really knows what they heard or saw, paid attention to, engaged with and responded to. Only they know what is and was important to them. And, until today, we have had limited methods of capturing that information.

For the most part, the methodologies that have been developed have been primarily intra-media comparisons—what channel on the TV, what magazine of the 10,000 or more alternatives, what intersection for the outdoor sign and so on. Thus, while we might know what television program to buy and place commercials based on demographics, we don't know if another media form was in use at the same time. And if simultaneous media usage was occurring, which of the media forms was receiving the most attention. Further, we don't know which media form has the most impact on the consumer, that is, which one influences the consumer the most by product category.

The new BIGresearch system, which deals directly with consumers, their media usage and their media interests begins to solve some of these media choice and allocation problems, as has been illustrated in the previous chapters.

Thus, media planners can begin to move from media distribution planning to media consumption analysis. That's the first big value of the new BIGresearch and SIMM system.

Overcoming the Practical Application Issues

There are many consumer-led methods of measuring media audiences on an individual basis. The problem with these is, however, that knowing that the most valuable audience is, for example, a "blue-blood, higher income, soccer mom" doesn't help the media planner or buyer very much. Media organizations have or are able to share only limited amounts of information on their audiences—primarily geographic and, by inference, demographic. Thus, the more finely the advertising planner is able to identify the target audience, the less valuable that information becomes. Trying to cut one's way through the jungle with a scalpel is a very difficult task and generally not very successful.

Given this inter-media need, and that only intra-media data is generally available, the BIGresearch studies become even more important. We understand the restrictions on what media planners and buyers can do with the media information available now. That is why the new BIGresearch planning approach is such a revolutionary idea, and why we have created the new concept of media generations. It is a methodology that marries the available data with consumer-provided input that truly enables the media planner and buyer to take out much of the previous guesswork and intuition that has prevailed in media allocation.

Media Generations as the New Media Planning Approach

In the previous chapters, we have shown the differences in media consumption and influence by media generations and their application to media planning and strategy. The media generations methodology offers a foundation to address the inter-media comparison allocation problem based upon media influence. It also contributes to a better understanding of intra-media issues as well.

The media generations can be understood by the different styles of media consumption and usage that are found in the marketplace. This draws on the central idea that the media usage style a consumer has, depends upon the media and cultural environment in place when they grew up.

The Silent Generation, born before 1945, grew up during World War II. Today, they are either retired or approaching retirement. They watch the most television of any of the generations and believe that newspapers are the most influential medium. They are the least interested in activities and other outside activities. Relatively, they are interested in gardening and travel.

The Mass Generation, born between 1946 and 1956, grew up during the start of the Cold War and the rise of network television. This generation corresponds to the leading baby boomers who grew up during the expansion of over-the-air broadcast television and the traditional three networks. Radio was dominated by middle-of-the-road talk radio when the leading boomers were children. Thus, it is easy to name this generation the Mass Media Generation. They have the highest average income and claim newspapers and inserts as being relatively the most influential of all media forms. They differ from the Silent Generation in being more active in general and showing interest in outside-the-home activities such as going to movies, shopping and cooking.

Following the Mass Generation are the Trailing Boomers, that is, the children who grew up following Sputnik. They have been named the Space Generation. This Space Generation group was born between 1956 and 1964. Their common experience is the proliferation of media choices with FM radio, more magazine titles and the growth of cable television. The Space Generation is more interested in listening to music and going to movies than the Mass Generation. They also are the most interested in family activities. Many more media categories are reported to be highly influential with them, including inserts, television, reading an article, in-store promotion and direct mail.

The Hippie Generation consumers were born between 1965 and 1974. These are the children that grew up during the counter-culture movement and the Vietnam War. They are also referred to as Thirteenth Generation. They have the highest proportion of under-18 members of the household. Listening to music, surfing the internet and family activities are dominant activities. The most influential media are satellite, terrestrial and web radio, coupons, and newspapers.

The trailing edge is commonly referred to as Generation X and is named here as the Computer Generation, born between 1975 and 1987. This generation saw the introduction and early acceptance of the personal computer. They are the most active of any generation. They add socializing with family and friends to their activities. Relatively speaking, most media categories are influential in their eyes, with the exception of television.

The last, and youngest generation, born after 1988, generally referred to as Millennials, grew up with the internet. The Internet Generation is dominated by listening to music, surfing the internet and going to movies. The Internet Generation has seen the digital revolution and the beginnings and acceptance of social networking media. The most influential media include texting, video games and instant messaging.

Using the Media Generations in Planning and Buying

Allocating media spending by media influence against the appropriate media generations is a way to dramatically increase the effectiveness and efficiency of marketing communication. Using media influence allows the allocation of spending across media categories, not just within them. While that changes a long-held tradition, it is a methodology media planners and buyers should welcome.

The media generations and influences are dynamic since everyone in every audience is continuously aging. They must, therefore, be continuously monitored and adaptations made to those changes. Differences in markets and product categories must also be measured and considered. Cultural differences must be studied as well, and will be the subject of future monographs.

A Final Thought

It is self-evident that media planning and buying cannot continue to use the methods, systems and technologies that were developed in the 1970s and 1980s. While they are comfortable and are the current currency in media allocation, these methods are as obsolete as carbon paper. Many media planners and buyers are acting as agents for their clients. Thus, they have a fiduciary responsibility to allocate the finite corporate resources in the most effective and efficient manner possible. We believe the material in this monograph will help improve that capability and generate greater returns for both the marketer and the media groups.

About the Authors

Martin P. Block is a Professor in the Integrated Marketing Communications Division of the Medill School at Northwestern University. He is currently sector head for Entertainment and Gaming. He teaches graduate level marketing research, sales promotion, advertising, and direct marketing courses. Previously, Martin was a Professor and Chairperson of the Department of Advertising at Michigan State University. Martin is co-author of Media Generations (BIGresearch, 2008), Analyzing Sales Promotion (Dartnell, 1994), Business-to-Business Market Research, (Thomson, 2007). His recent chapter "Post Promotion Evaluation" appears in The Power of Marketing at-Retail (POPAI, 2008). He was also co-author of Cable Advertising: New Ways to New Business (Prentice-Hall, 1987). He has published in academic research journals and trade publications. He has been the principal investigator on several Federally funded research projects and has served as a consultant to the Federal Trade Commission (FTC).

Don E. Schultz is Professor (Emeritus-in-Service) of Integrated Marketing Communications at Northwestern University, Evanston, IL. He is also President of Agora, Inc., a global marketing, communication and branding consulting firm also headquartered in Evanston, IL. Schultz lectures, conducts seminars and conferences and consults on five continents. He is the author of eighteen books and over 100 trade, academic and professional articles. He is a featured columnist

in MARKETING NEWS and MARKETING MANAGEMENT.
He was the founding editor of THE JOURNAL OF DIRECT
MARKETING. Schultz is recognized as a leading authority on
new developments in marketing and communication and has helped
develop the Integrated Marketing and Integrated Marketing Communication concepts around the world along with pioneering work in
marketing accountability, branding, internal marketing and marketing
metrics/ROI.

BIGresearch is a consumer intelligence firm providing behavioral
insights in areas of products and services, retail, financial services, automotive, and media. Their Consumer Intentions and Actions (CIA) Survey monitors more than 8,000 consumers each month and delivers fresh,
demand-based information on where the retail consumer is shopping
and their changing behavior. BIGresearch's Simultaneous Media Usage
Survey (SIMM) of more than 15,000 consumers is conducted twice
each year and gauges consumption across media, products and services.
BIGresearch's large sample sizes and methodology provides highly
accurate consumer information with a margin of error of +/- 1 percent.
www.bigresearch.com